Aircraft & Legend

MESSERSCHMITT

Bf 109

Aircraft & Legend
MESSERSCHMITT
Bf 109

HEINZ J. NOWARRA

Foulis

Haynes

A **FOULIS** Aviation Book

First published 1986 in German by Motorbuch Verlag as 'Die 109' by Heinz J. Nowarra

English language edition published 1989

Published by:
Haynes Publishing Group
Sparkford, Nr. Yeovil, Somerset BA22 7JJ, England

Haynes Publications Inc.
861 Lawrence Drive, Newbury Park,
California 91320, USA

British Library Cataloguing in Publication Data
Nowarra, Heinz J. (Heinz Joachim), *1912-*
  Messerschmitt Me109.
  1. Messerschmitt BF 109 aeroplanes, history
  I. Title
  623.74'64
  ISBN .i.0-85429-729-4

Library of Congress catalog card number 89-84707

Editor: Robin Read
Cover illustration: Philip Oliver
Translator: Ian Gordon
Printed in England by: J. H. Haynes & Co. Ltd

Contents

Foreword

The Messerschmitt 109 inspired countless articles in the specialist press and many books about it have been written both here and abroad since the end of the Second World War. So why another book? After writing two books on the Me 109 at an earlier date I decided to write another book on the same subject because I realised that all the books which had so far appeared had concentrated on the aircraft itself at the expense of the events – and the 109 *must* be seen in context. Without neglecting the technical development of the 109 and its successors and design projects 209, 309, 409, 509, 609 and 155, this book attempts to fill in the historical background which influenced the development of these types and to depict the inter-relationship between the development of the use of fighter aircraft in general and this, the most flown fighter. Although many fighter pilots flew the Fw 190, the Ta 152 or jet fighters, at some time all of them would have piloted the 109. It is my hope that the documentation in this book will fill out the historical and technical detail for all those who are interested in the 109, whatever their specific interest.

On my own I could never have managed to provide all the material, so I would like to

thank all those who have made this book possible by making available photographs, documentation and other information. In particular I would like to thank:

Gebhard Aders, Cologne; Peter M Bowers, Seattle, USA; Peter Buchar, Prague, Czechoslovakia; Oberst (retd) Harry von Bülow; G. van Dessel, Belgium; Fritz Hahn, Oberkochen; Rainer Haufschild, Berlin; Armin Kerle, Böblingen; Wolfgang Koch, Berlin; Marian Krzyzan, Zielona Gora, Poland; Ernst Maison, JG 74 'Mölders'; Günther Ott, Berlin; Peter Petrick, Berlin; Peter Pletschacher, Munich; Thijs Postma, Hoofddorp, Holland; Helmuth Roosenboom, Bremen; Dipl.-Ing. Franz Selinger, Ulm; Jay P. Spenser, Smithsonian Institution, USA; Lt Knut Store, Norway; Dr Fritz Stormer, Pinneberg; Col (retd) Raymond Toliver, Calif. USA; US Air Force, Washington DC, USA; André Ver Elst, Zemst, Belgium, Messerschmitt-Bölkow-Blohm, Ottobrunn; Walter Zuerl, Steinebach/W; Volker Reschke, Korschenbroich, Leo Schmitt, Mendig; Konrad Molin, Vienna, and Dr R. Gentilli, Florence.

Heinz J Nowarra
Harreshausen

Background to the 109

The story of the Messerschmitt Bf 109 (technically the correct designation of the Me 109) is so closely connected with the designer himself that we need to be aware of the life of Professor Dr Ing. e.h. Willy Messerschmitt and his work if we are to understand the story of his famous aircraft. Whilst still a student at Munich Technische Hochschule in 1923 Willy Messerschmitt had founded the Messerschmitt Flugzeugbau company in Bamberg. His interest in building aircraft went back much further, however. He was born on 26 June 1898, the son of a wine merchant in Frankfurt/Main. In 1909 he visited the international air show at Frankfurt and immediately began to build model aircraft – he was then 12. In the First World War he was initially with a mortar unit but in 1918 he joined the Schleißheim Flying School, the 'birthplace of military aviation in Bavaria'. After the war he built his first gliders, working with Harth, a government architect. These gliders were flown in the Rhön competitions. In 1922 he split from Harth and one year later founded his company in Bamberg. His first major success was the diminutive M 18 passenger aircraft. He had been commissioned to build it by Theo Croneiß, who was at that time in charge of Sportflug GmbH at Nuremberg/Fürth. To facilitate the project the Bamberg factory and Sportflug GmbH

amalgamated on 25 March 1926 to become Messerschmitt Flugzeugbau GmbH. In 1927 he produced his first passenger aircraft of any size, the M 20. This aircraft was bought by Lufthansa. But there was a design failing in this aircraft which was to recur in Messerschmitt's designs: the tail was too weak. After a number of crashes the M 20s were only permitted to be used for cargo. In the same year Messerschmitt entered into a working agreement with the Bayrische Flugzeugwerke (Bavarian Aircraft Works) in Augsburg. In 1929 the Stromeyer-Michel-Raulino Finance Group (Frau Messerschmitt's maiden name was Raulino) together with Messerschmitt, acquired a majority of shares in Bayrische Flugzeugwerke AG (BFW) which had previously belonged to the state of Bavaria and the German Reich. The co-operation resulting from the working agreement of the previous year could now become even closer. The capital, which at the time was RM 400,000 was increased to RM 5.6 million by 1939, with 88 per cent of it belonging to the Michel-Raulino-Messerschmitt Group. But along the way times were hard and led to the collapse of BFW in 1931. Messerschmitt Flugzeugbau, however, continued. The most serious crisis was the threat that the workshops would be confiscated and this was only averted by the intervention of the National Socialist Town Council under the chairmanship of Rudolf Hess, later to become Hitler's deputy. After the bankruptcy proceedings were concluded on 27 April 1933, BFW was able to go back into aircraft production. The new owners needed the works for the construction of military aircraft. In a *Deutsche Arbeitsfront* pamphlet of that time it actually states: 'After the National Socialists came to power it was primarily Reichminister Rudolph Hess, deputy to the Führer, who was responsible for supporting and promoting the Messerschmitt factory. Hess, well known as a pilot in the First World War, had bought himself an M 23 and used it for his travels during the campaign in his role as former private secretary to the Führer. Rudolf Hess won the Zugspitzflug in 1934 flying an M 35.'

Messerschmitt was responsible for many innovations which we now take for granted in modern aircraft construction. From the start he was an exponent of the low-wing cantilever monoplane at a time when virtually everyone saw the biplane as the way forward.

In a lecture to the Deutschen Akademie für Luftfahrtforschung (Academy for Aviation Research) in November 1937 Messerschmitt summed up his aims and the tasks which he had undertaken in his work. He showed how different had been the development of high speed aircraft in Germany and in other countries. His first attempt at exploiting all the findings of research into high speed flight was the M 29 low-wing monoplane, built in 1932 with the modest means at his disposal prior to 1933. Its 150 PS produced a maximum speed of 165 mph and a landing speed of 40 mph. Signs of weakness were already appearing in Messerschmitt design, however; on 8 August 1932 an M 29 crashed, followed on the next day by the crash of a second M 29. Whilst approaching Schleißheim the tailplane began to vibrate and then broke off and the wings failed. The pilot Reinhold Poss and his passenger Starchinsky were both killed outright.

The aerobatic M 35 low-wing monoplane was a great success especially when piloted by the German aerobatic champion Willy Stör. With its cantilever telescopic undercarriage legs the M 35 was the most elegant aircraft of its time. What was particularly interesting in this aircraft was the impressive power/weight ratio and its harmless spin characteristics.

In 1934 Messerschmitt, who had so far included wood in the construction of his aircraft, went over to 100 per cent metal. The first all-metal aircraft, which can be seen as the direct predecessor to the Me 109, was the M 37 which was redesignated Bf 108 after the Reichskommissariat für Luftfahrt (later known as the Reichsluftfahrt-Ministerium-RLM) had introduced the type list. The aircraft had been built for the Europa-Rundflug 1934 (Tour of Europe) and was of seminal importance in the development of the modern touring aircraft. Indeed it can even be seen as the prototype of the modern touring aircraft because few changes to the design of the Bf 108 would be needed even today. The version of the Bf 108 used in the Europa-Rundflug 1934 used the Hirth Hm 8U 250 PS engine, and was also tested with the Argus As 17 of 220 PS. In other respects it was largely similar to the Bf 108B which went into series production, powered by the 240 PS Argus As 10c engine. The Bf 108B was somewhat larger than the Bf 108A and had additional glazing in the luggage compartment. It was low-wing cantilever monoplane with a two-part metal wing.

The short centre section was incorporated in the fuselage construction. The wing was a torsionally stiff single-spar design and had landing flaps between the ailerons and the fuselage, and also leading edge slots across two-thirds of the wingspan. The fuselage was of monocoque construction in metal, the tail and fin being all metal, but the rudder and elevator were a fabric-covered metal structure and aerodynamically balanced. The Bf 108 had a retractable undercarriage with telescopic cantilever legs that were retracted outwards into the wings by turning a handle. The tail wheel was not retractable. The aircraft had four seats, two at the front having dual controls. The luggage space was behind the rear seats. In 1941 some Bf 108Cs were delivered with the Hirth HM 512 400 PS engine turning an Argus variable-pitch propeller. Altogether 885 Bf 108s were built. When war broke out they were used as a communications aircraft by many Luftwaffe squadrons. After 1945 the French firm SNCA du Nord, which had build the Bf 108 under licence, built another 285 aircraft (some with Renault engines), which were known as the Nord 1000 Pingouin (Penguin). They also developed a tricycle undercarriage Me 208 but only two were built. Nord, however, built the Me 208 in limited numbers as the Nord 1101 Noralpha powered by a Renault engine. Some years ago in West Germany there were plans for production of an updated Bf 108, but the project failed.

Some of the design features of the Bf109 can already be seen in the Bf 108 A

1. Heinkel versus Messerschmitt: Competition to build the Luftwaffe 'Standard Fighter'

The Reichskommissariat für Luftfahrt (German Aviation Commission) was set up on 2 February 1933 under Hermann Göring and it became generally apparent that the signal had been given for the rearmament of the German Reich, with particular emphasis on air power. On 15 May 1933 the next step was taken when the Luftschutzamt der Reichswehr (roughly, Air Defence Bureau) which before 1933 had been the basis for a Luftwaffe, was transferred to the newly formed Reichsluftfahrt-Ministerium (German Air Ministry). This consisted of the various flying schools and the three so called *Reklamestaffelm* ('publicity squadrons') set up in 1930, and one marine squadron which still had no genuine operational significance. In terms of personnel there were 120 trained fighter pilots in Lipezk, the secret Luftwaffe base in the Soviet Union, 80 observers and 200 other pilots. The fighter aircraft at Lipezk were the Fokker D XIII and within the German Reich the Arado Ar 65 and the Heinkel HD 38 seaplane single-seat fighter. They were all biplanes. The first RLM rearmament programme envisaged the availability of 1000 aircraft by 1 October 1935. These numbers were shortly to be revised upwards. As early as 1 July 1934 there was an aircraft procurement programme requiring the construction of 4021 aircraft.

As this book deals mainly with fighter aircraft the numbers given here refer specifically to such types. The programme included the construction initially of 19 Ar 64s, 85 Ar 65s, 141 He 51s, 14 He 51Ws, He 38Ws. By the end of 1934, however, only 19 Ar 64s and 84 Ar 65s had actually been delivered. The reason for this was mainly due to a shortage of engines. Engine problems were to haunt the German military aviation scene right up to 1945.

In March the creation of the secret Luftwaffe was gradually revealed. The German civilian pilot school at Schleißheim became a fighter pilot school and the publicity squadron in central Germany became Jagdgeschwader 132 in Döberitz.

Major Robert Ritter von Greim was appointed Inspekteur der Jadflieger. Born in 1892 in Bayreuth, he had been awarded the *Pour le Mérite,* been a fighter pilot with 28 kills and one of the first supporters of Hitler. In February 1936 he was succeeded by Ernst Udet who had been promoted to the rank of Oberst on 1 June 1935. Although born in Frankfurt, Udet's home was Munich. On 9 June 1936 Udet was appointed Head of the Technisches Amt (technical office) in the RML and so became a decisive influence on the development of German rearmament in the air.

In the middle of 1936 fighter strength was

**Messerschmitt
Bf 109 V1 D-IABI**

**Messerschmitt and
Hubert Bauer 1938**

considerably increased through the creation of two Geschwaderstäbe and four new Jagdgruppen (fighter groups). They were the Stab (staff) of Jagdgeschwader 132 'Richthofen' at Döberitz and Jagdgeschwader (JG) 134 in Dortmund, to which I./JG134, II./JG 134 in Werl and III./JG 134 created in February (first at Lippstadt, then Cologne and Düsseldorf) were subordinate. In addition I./JG 232 was set up at Bernburg. And finally there was the coastal fighter wing of Küstenjagdgruppe 136 at Jever.

The first rearmament programme of the RLM in 1934 (mentioned above) was the basis for the development of new fighter aircraft. In his role as Inspekteur der Jagdflieger, Udet had reformulated the specifications for fighter aircraft as early as 1936. He pushed for the re-equipment of the fighter units whose He 51s and Ar 68s were obsolete. Now for the first time there was a call for two different types of fighter aircraft: the 'light fighter' to be highly manoeuvrable and with a maximum speed between 310 and 375 mph, and the 'heavy fighter' which was to be a twin-engined aircraft with a range of 1,250 miles and maximum speed of 310 to 340 mph. These decisions on fighter aircraft policy were crucial as we shall see when they later prove to be so disastrous. The outcome of this policy was the Messerschmitt Bf 109 and the Bf 110. When Udet became Head of the Technisches Amt of the RLM on 9 June 1936 he was in a position to promote these ideas energetically. Heinkel, Arado and Focke-Wolf received development contracts for the new 'light fighter'. Bayrische Flugzeugwerke did not receive a development contract but began to develop their design, initially without official support. The M 21 training biplane and the two-engined M 22 bomber, which had been developed for the Reichswehr by BFW

before 1933, had not won many supporters. In addition there were the crashes of the M 29 light aircraft and the M 20 passenger aircraft, which had increased distrust of Messerschmitt's designs in the RLM. Nevertheless, a development contract was eventually awarded to Messerschmitt at the time when his competitors were already building their prototypes. In April 1934 Messerschmitt's team, consisting of Robert Lusser, project Head: Richard Bauer, Head of Design; and Hubert Bauer, who was at that time Head of Production, began work on the light fighter aircraft under Messerschmitt's personal direction. The team set out with the design concept of the smallest possible airframe for the most powerful German aircraft engine being developed. These design criteria led, of necessity, to a high wing-loading, so it was necessary to build in the maximum number of lift-creating devices. These included automatic leading-edge slats to maintain aileron effectiveness at low speeds, large slotted flaps and slotted ailerons. As with the Bf 108, Messerschmitt decided on a low-wing cantilever monoplane with single-spar wings with torsionally stiff leading edge. As the intended Daimler-Benz engine was not yet available, a British Rolls-Royce Kestrel V developing 695 PS at take-off was installed.

What were competitors building in the meantime? It turned out that all three designers, – Kurt Tank, technical manager at Focke-Wulf, Walter Blume at Arado and Professor Hertel at Heinkel – had different ideas on the development of a 'light fighter'. Tank used his lightweight Fw 56 single-seater as the starting point and developed an all-metal high-wing monoplane with struts and an undercarriage which retracted backwards into the fuselage. The engine was the new Junkers Jumo 210A with

Rivals to the Bf 109 V1: Arado Ar 80 V1 (top), Heinkel He 112 V1 (centre) and Focke-Wulf Fw 159 V1 (below)

take-off power of 610 PS. The undercarriage caused serious problems from the start because Focke-Wulf had no experience of retractable undercarriages at that time. When Captain Wolfgang Stein took off for his maiden flight in the Fw 159 V1 in 1935 everything seemed to go well to begin with. But as he came in to land and touched down the undercarriage collapsed completely. It was necessary to rebuild the aircraft for the flight trials at the Rechlin Luftwaffe Test Centre.

Things were very different at Arado. Walter Blume believed that if the aircraft were built light enough a retractable undercarriage was not necessary, providing that sufficient attention was paid to an aerodynamic fairing. However, as Arado had no experience of all-metal construction, the aircraft ended up too heavy. Although the Ar 80 VI had the first-class British Rolls-Royce 'Kestrel V', it was not enough to make up for the weaknesses of the aircraft.

Heinkel's design also used the British Rolls-Royce engine which was later fitted in the prototype of the Bf 109. The Heinkel He 112 V1 was an all-metal cantilever low-wing monoplane with broad-track undercarriage. It did originally have an open cockpit but this was easily converted to a closed canopy. The basic design of the He 112 stemmed from the brothers Walter and Siegfried Günter, as can be seen in its similarity to the He 70 and He 111.

In the meantime Bf 109 V1, D-IABI, was completed in May 1935. The maiden flight took place at Augsburg at the end of 1935 with Hans-Dietrich Knoetzsch at the controls. The manufacturer's tests were completed at the beginning of October and Knoetzsch then delivered the aircraft to Rechlin with an intermediate landing at Leipzig-Mockau airfield. On landing the Bf 109 demonstrated for the first time a weakness which was to plague it throughout its whole career: the undercarriage collapsed. The aircraft was repaired and then taken to Travemünde where the flight trials were to take place at the end of October.

A decision had to be made between the Bf 109 and the He 112. Comparison of the two aircraft showed that the Bf 109 was faster in level flight than the He 112 and also climbed faster. On the other hand the He 112 had the advantage of excellent ground-handling because of its broad-track undercarriage which was very important for front line operations. The Technisches Amt of the RLM decided to have ten test aircraft built of each type and then to make their final decision. Messerschmitt built ten of these aircraft to his initial design without introducing any major changes other than improvements, reinforcement modifications and installing more powerful engines. There was a crisis at Heinkel on which Ernst Heinkel comments in his memoirs: 'It was Hertel who in constructing the He 112 first revealed his predelection for endless changes, experiments and innovations, and so he was responsible for the He 112 being ready after the Me 109. He was responsible for example, for the fact, that it had to be handed over to the first Luftwaffe Test Engineer without the automatic undercarriage mechanism fully installed. The pilot had to operate the hydraulic pump manually to retract the undercarriage. When he climbed out of the aircraft on landing he was cursing and sweating profusely'

It was little wonder then that the Rechlin engineers were unenthusiastic about the He 112. Udet himself flew the He 112 himself a few times – and then decided to make the Bf 109 the standard fighter for the Luftwaffe.

Critical considerations included the fact

Bf 109 V3, Works No.
760 (top), Bf 109 V4
(B-01) Works No. 878
(centre) and Bf 109
V5 Works No. 879
(bottom)

that the Bf 109 was more suited to series production and that with wings detached it could be transported on its own undercarriage (a design specification which the He 112 did not meet). The wing was attached to the fuselage with three easily removable rigging pins. Situated under the fuselage firewall was the fitting for the telescopic undercarriage leg, which also served as the pickup point for the forward auxiliary spar and the lower strut of the engine mounting – an imaginative design feature. But having the undercarriage attached to the fuselage meant a narrow undercarriage track and that remained one of the weaknesses of the 109 tolerated only because of other overwhelming advantages in the design.

At that time it was too early to recognise that the decision to concentrate on one aircraft type would later prove dangerous. In the disappointed Heinkel's opinion, Udet saw the advantage of his decision in terms of the rational use of materials and labour. The danger that vast resources might be invested in just one aircraft type, a type which was then in 1940 during the Battle of Britain to suffer from inadequate range, was underestimated.

Bf 109 V1, D-IABI, was works no. 758. Bf 109 V2, D-IILU and V3, D-IOQY, were works nos. 759 and 760. Unlike VI these were powered by the Jumo 210 A. These three experimental aircraft were the only examples of the planned 'A' series which was abandoned because of its weak armament of only two MG 17s (7.9 mm). Only Bf 109 V3 had this armament. The V2 flew for the first time in January 1936, and the V3 in June of the same year.

The ten test aircraft manufactured under the RLM contract represent the pre-series Bf 109 B. The prototype for the B-1 series was B-01 with the designation Bf 109 V4. It was works no. 878 and bore the registration D-IALY. It was followed by V5, works No. 879, D-IEKS (or D-ILGO?) and V6, works no. 880, D-IHHB. They are numbers -02 and -03 of the B-0 series. The B-1 differed from the A-version in the installation of a third fixed weapon which was installed between the cylinder blocks of the V engine and fired through the hollow propeller spinner which was brought in line by a reduction gear box. Both the other weapons were above the engine and fired through the propeller using the old Fokker MG synchronisation system of 1915. Originally an additional MG 17 was intended as the motor cannon. Later experiments were made using an MG/FFM (20mm calibre) but these had to be discontinued as the weapon proved to be unreliable. The B-1 was powered by the improved Jumo 210 Da with 650 PS at take-off. The B-1 was only built in a short series. The first aircraft went to Jagdgeschwader 132 "Richthofen".

V1 and V6 and B-1 had wooden propellers, manufactured by the firm of G. Schwarz in Berlin-Waidmannslust. Some of these aircraft then went to Spain for service testing by Jagdgruppe J88 of the Condor Legion in Spain. This had proved necessary after the Soviet Union had supplied the Republican Air Force in Spain with modern Polikarpow I-15 and I-16 ("Rata") fighters, which were in every way superior to the Heinkel He 51 flown by the German fighter pilots in Spain. The 1. Staffel of J 88 was the first to be equipped with the Bf 109 B-1.

In the meantime back in Germany factory test flying and service evaluation of the Bf 109 V5 and V6 had been completed and these were the prototypes for the B-2 series.

The first Bf 109 B-1s on the airfield at Augsburg ➤

The main difference between B-1 and B-2 was in the power plant. Junkers had produced an improved version of the Jumo 210, the Eabis, which produced 680 PS at take-off. Performance in the air could be improved still further by using Hamilton (USA) variable pitch two-blade metal propellers which were made under licence in the Vereinigte Deutsche Metallwerke (VDM) in Frankfurt-Heddernheim. The Junkers Motorenwerke (Jumo) in Dessau-Alten were able to further increase the performance of the Jumo 210 in the G version to 700PS. The take-off weight of the Bf 109 B-2 was 2,200 kg. The standard version of the aircraft could reach 276 mph at 13,100 ft altitude. At a lower flying weight, ie. after some of the fuel had been consumed, the maximum performance of 292 mph at 12,100 ft.

A total of 52 aircraft in the B-1 and B-2 series were sent to Spain and flown successfully by Staffel 1 and 2 of JG 88. They were later replaced by aircraft of the E-1 series and then handed over to General Franco's Spanish National Air Force.

Test flying in Germany and operational use in Spain confirmed time and time again that the Bf 109 was not without problems. The Luftwaffe Test Centre at Rechlin and the Messerschmitt factories in Augsburg (as the Bayrische Flugzeugwerke were called after 1938) were constantly trying to improve the Bf 109 and eliminate the difficulties which kept occurring. Two major problems plagued the designers. The first was vibration of the tail when the engine was running at full power. Earlier Messerschmitt designs had proved to have a weak tail design, as has already been mentioned. The second difficulty was the undercarriage, a problem that was never really solved. The undercarriage had a tendency to collapse and the aircraft also ground-looped on take-off and landing. This tendency was apparent in initial test flights, during proving flights of series production aircraft and, what was even worse, it also occurred in service with the Luftwaffe and caused a disproportionately high number of aircraft to be out of service. Whilst working at the Junkers-Werft Leipzig-Mokkau at the Erla-Werken at Leipzig-Heiterblick, (the largest factory producing the Bf 109 under licence) the author witnessed a dozen Bf 109 undercarriage failures on that airfield on one day. Many aircraft would take off reasonably well, fly a circuit and then settle down to their approach to land. On touchdown one undercarriage leg would sometimes fail and the aircraft would then swing round and do a ground loop, as it is called. It would then lie there with a damaged wing and bent propeller; useless.

One modification which had both positive and also negative results was the installation of an automatic leading edge slot. These slots opened automatically below a certain speed and maintained the airflow over the wing. As the speed increased the slot automatically returned to the closed position. In a dogfight the 109 would often go into a steep turn and sometimes the airflow over the inner wing would be slow enough for the slots to be extended. This resulted in a flick roll which took the pilot unawares. If the aircraft was high enough it was no great problem to regain control by applying opposite aileron and rudder. At low altitude however this led to the aircraft crashing and

Top: Bf 109 B-1. This aircraft is still painted in the earlier segment-camouflage. Below: One of the first Bf 109 B-1s, sent to Spain ➤

18

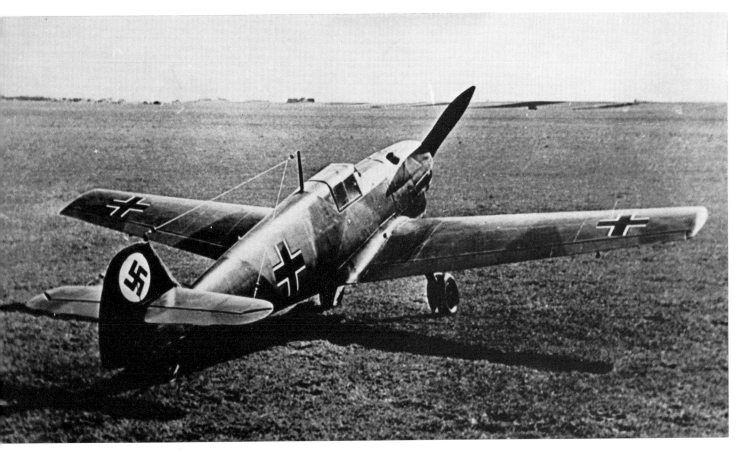

Bf 109 V6 (B-03) Works No. 880

Bf 109 B-2 during flight tests

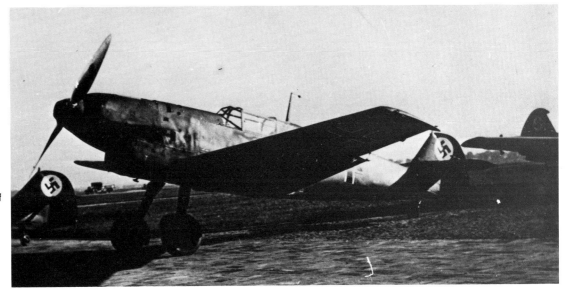

Photographed at
Hage in Holstein:
Top: Bf 109 B-2 of
II./JG 132. Centre:
Ju 52, Ju 34, Fw 56,
He 51 and Bf 109 B-2
of I. and II./JG 132.
Lower: Firing tests of
a Bf 109 B-2 of II./JG
132

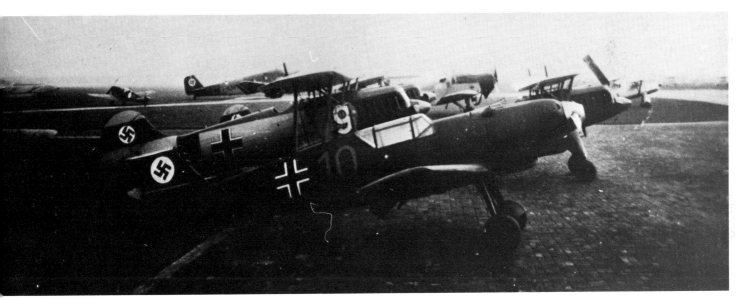

Bf 109 B-2 of 2.(J) Tr.
GR. 186

Hauptmann Stormer
of Stab Tr. Gr. 186
with a Bf 109 B-2. The
Träger-Gruppe 186
(Aircraft Carrier
Wing) was intended
for the
"Graf-Zeppelin"
aircraft carrier which
was never completed

Fitters of JG 2
"Richthofen" during
the occupation of
Czechoslovakia,
Karlsbad 1939

22

Bf 109 B-2 of Jagdgruppe J 88 of the Condor Legion

II/JG 76 with two Bf 109 B-2s in the Spring of 1939

to fatalities. The other shortcomings of the Bf 109 became especially apparent when the twelve B-2s returned from Spain to Germany and after the fighter pilots of the Legion Condor had filed their reports.

In the meantime two other aircraft of the B-0 series had been turned into test aircraft. B-04, works no. 881, D-IJHA, became Bf 109 V7 and B-05, works no. 882, D-IPLU, became V8. They were identical with the B-2 apart from armament; became the prototypes of a new C series and were completed in 1937.

As the motor cannon firing through the centre of the propeller spinner had proved to be too unreliable and the Inspektion der Jagdflieger had demanded increased armament, two non-synchronised MG 17s were later built into the wing of the Bf 109 C-1. Tests on the Bf 107 V7 with this armament had proved satisfactory. In the V8 the problem of inadequate ventilation for the motor cannon had finally been solved. The short C-2 series, which was equivalent to the V8, was then equipped with the following MG 17s: one in the engine, two above the engine and two in the wings. In all 12 of the C series were then sent to Spain for front line testing. The Bf 109 was already on the way to becoming a first class unbeatable fighter but it was still short of the necessary 1,000 PS engine. Berger and Nallinger, both *Diplomingenieure*, had been working on the development of such an engine at Daimler-Benz AG in Stuttgart-Untertürkheim since 1932. The engine in question was the DB 600, a liquid cooled inverted V12 engine which was well suited to being aerodynamically faired in as it used reduction gears and a hollow shaft which also permitted the installation of a motor cannon. Initial test versions produced 800 PS; soon they succeeded in increasing power output to 910 PS. The last versions of this engine, Ga

and Ha, even developed as much as 1,050 PS. The Bf 109 V11 (B-08) and V12 (B-09) were the first aircraft to be equipped with the DB 600A, which was a carburettor engine. Although a number of DB 600s were built they reacted to negative g values in flight by cutting out. The DB 600 never reached the production figures of its successor, the DB 601, which was a fuel injection engine. It can be seen that the DB 600 was only an interim solution from the fact that the D series was fitted with the Jumo 210D. Bf 109 B9 (B-06) and V10 (B-07) were not used for development or testing but for a special purpose which will be revealed later. The last aircraft of the B-0 pre-series, the B-010, D-IPKY, had a chequered career. It was fitted with the DB 600A and flown as Bf 109 V13, was later the first to be fitted with the DB 601A, and now became the first aircraft of the E-0 series, E-01. Bf 109 V14, D-ISLU became E-02, also powered by the DB 600A.

Bf 109 V9, V10, V13 and three Bf 109 B-2s stole the show at an Aviation Week which the newly-formed German Luftwaffe offered to the world at Zürich-Dübendorf airfield from 23 July to 1 August 1937. It was the annual international aviation meeting at Zürich which had now been running for fifteen years. This was the first time that Germany had taken part. Not surprisingly, aviation journalists and military aircraft experts from all over the world raced to Zürich. The Germans were triumphant throughout. Major Hans Seidemann had a comfortable win in the Alpine Race flying the Bf 109 V9 (B-06) works no. 883. The team prize in this event was won by the German team of Hauptmann Schleif, Hauptmann Restemeier and Leutnant "Hannes" Trautloft, later Kommodore of JG 54, each flying a Bf 109 B-2. The climb and dive competition

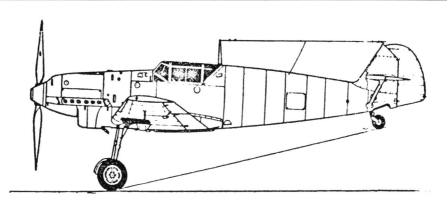

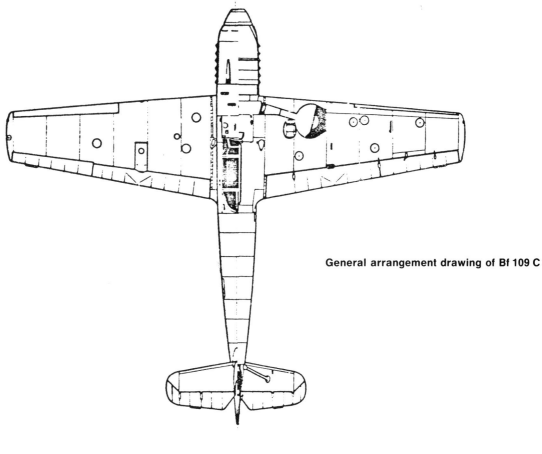

General arrangement drawing of Bf 109 C

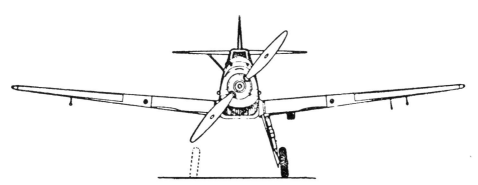

25

Bf 109 C-1. The leading edge openings for the enclosed machine guns are clearly visible

Bf 109 Cs of JG 134 at Bernburg 1938

Opposite: Three air-to-air shots of Bf 109 C ➤

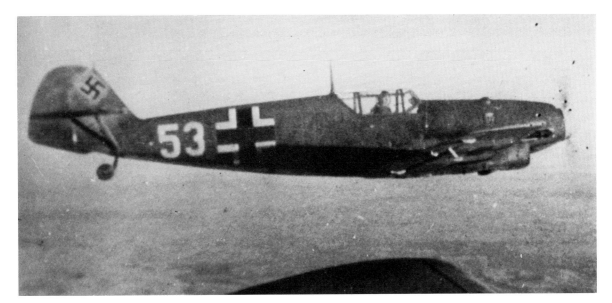

Left, Bf 109 C-2 of the 2. Staffel of JG 71 on manoeuvres. Fitters overhauling the engine and fuelling up.

Bf 109 C-2 of 2./JG 71. Above: Armourers loading the MG 17. Below: The same aircraft is pushed to the hangar across the wet tarmac

Right top: Bf 109 C-2 of the fighter training school Jagdfliegerschule Aspern. Below: Bf 109 C-2 at fighter training school Jagdschule Zerbst

With the arrival of the D and E series the Bf 109 Cs went to training schools. These photographs show flying operations at the fighter training school Jagdfliegerschule Werneuchen. These aircraft already had the new camouflage

was won by the Rechlin test pilot Francke flying the Bf 109 V13. Only one pilot had bad luck: Generalluftzeugmeister Ernst Udet. He found the complicated techniques needed for coping with a high performance tuned engine rather daunting. After the engine in his Bf 109 V14 failed he made an emergency landing which wrecked the aircraft completely. Incidentally it is interesting to note that the German Do 17 MV-1 bomber was 25mph faster than the French Dewoitine D510 C.1 single-seat fighter.

People abroad were amazed. One journalist described it as "another aspect of the fascinating German miracle!" One foreign airforce officer who was not particularly well disposed to Germany said: "Look how the German Imperial Eagle has been re-established over the skies of Europe! Outstanding and significant!" The trick had worked. And yet at that time the Luftwaffe did not have adequate numbers of high performance fighters of that type nor of Do 17 MV-1 bombers. What could be better than continuing with tricks like that for political ends? Time was to prove that Hitler had others up his sleeve.

The Bf 109 V13 was returned to Messerschmitt and fitted with the new Daimler-Benz DB 601A which had been so drastically modified that it produced 1,650 PS, but not for long — or ever again! After once producing this power output they were a total write-off. On 11 November 1937 the chief test pilot of Bayrische Flugzeugwerke Dr Wurster flew the Bf 109 V13 over a measured distance of 3km (approximately 1.9 miles) at a height of 250 ft. In front of invited witnesses from the Fédération Aéronautique Internationale (FAI) he set up a world speed record for land-based aircraft of 379.4mph! The aviation reporter Heinz Bongartz wrote: "Zürich was an unexpected and spectacular proof of the dynamic rise of German aviation technology. This was further convincing proof. It was flown with a series production, standard version German Luftwaffe fighter." Comments like this abounded in the press in Germany and throughout the world. The intention was to create the impression that Germany had such a strong air force that it would be unwise to take it on.

The performance of the Bf 109 D-1 was not noticeably better than the previous series. The engine produced 680 PS at 13,120 ft and the aircraft attained a maximum speed of 286 mph. The armament was the same as the C-1-also four MG 17s. There was also little external difference. The V11 and the V12 had had certain similarities with the E series and now the D-1 had the same ducted radiator as the C-1.

Production of the Bf 109 D-1 which was originally at the BFW base at Augsburg, now spread to two additional branch factories in Regensburg and the Erla factory at Leipzig-Heiterblick. By the Autumn of 1938 it was already obvious that the development of the German Jagdwaffe had been stepped up considerably. The old biplanes, the He 51, Ar 65 and AR 68, were sent increasingly to pilot training schools. The returns from the Generalquartiermeister of the Luftwaffe indicated that there were already 583 Bf 109s in the field, with 510 of them operational. This number included series D with 471 aircraft (414 serviceable) and series B/C with 112 aircraft (96 serviceable). These figures also include aircraft flying with Legion Condor in Spain. In addition 12 Bf 109 D-1s were supplied to Switzerland and 3 to Hungary.

Behind the scenes there was competition, complete with propaganda methods, and this led to one of the major decision

Above: Bf 109 V11 and V12. Below: Propaganda photograph of the Bf 109 V12 with fictitious squadron markings

Top: Bf 109 V11 (B-08) Centre and below: Bf 109 D-1. These photographs show that outwardly there was very little difference between versions B, C and D

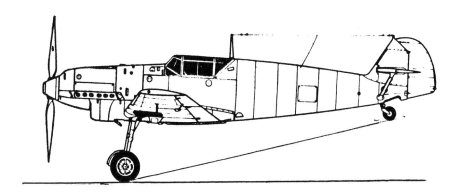

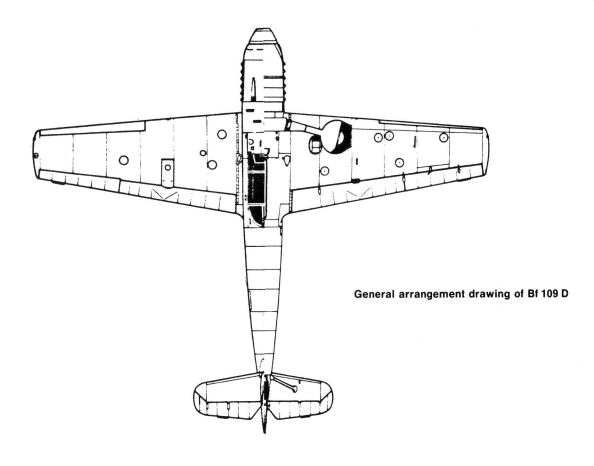

General arrangement drawing of Bf 109 D

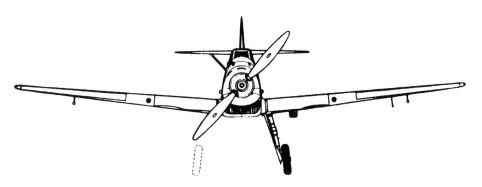

Bf 109 V14 (E-02) D-ISLU before painting

Udet just before his fateful flight in D-ISLU. On the left Dr. Wurster, on the right Engineer-General Lucht

36

Top and centre: Bf 109 V14 after
Udet's crash landing. Bottom: Udet
leaves the wreckage of D-ISLU,
annoyed at having been
responsible for the crash

Bf 109 V13, D-IPKY

Dipl.Ing Franke with the above aircraft, in which he came first at Zürich in the climbing and diving competition

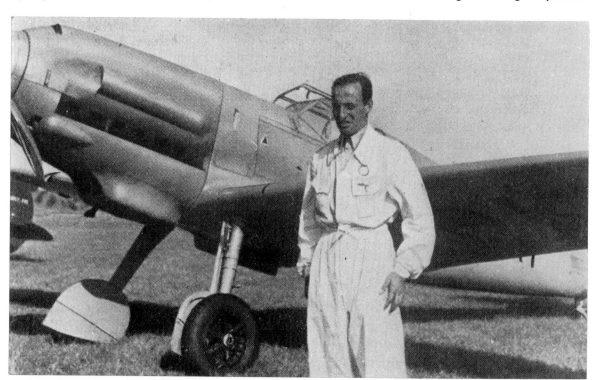

Bf 109 V9 with the winners of the formation event, from left to right: Trautloft, centre rear Restemeier, right Schleif

The formation flying Bf 109 B had no special markings

The Bf 109 V7 flew at Zürich under civil registration numbers

blunders in the history of German airpower.

Heinkel could not accept losing in the competition for the German fighter. In his memoirs he comments: "I should be untrue to myself if I were to deny that I was bitterly disappointed by the rejection of the He 112. My disappointment was all the greater because it had been my devout intention to produce a fast and maybe the fastest aircraft . . . 'the next fighter will be a Heinkel', I said to Udet. He was evasive and answered: 'In the Technisches Amt they are now of the opinion that aircraft manufacturers should specialise in particular types. That is a form of rationalisation. After its success with the Me 109, Messerschmitt is to be responsible for producing fighters. And after the He 111 you are to develop just bombers.'"

But Heinkel was determined to get into the fighter business whatever the obstacles in his path. After all he had been building fighters before Messerschmitt had even thought of it. He explained to Udet that he would offer a fighter test aircraft capable of 435 mph by the end of 1937. Udet laughed derisively. Needless to say Messerschmitt heard of Heinkel's plans. His reaction was to start work immediately on a new project, P.1059, later designated Me 209. Whereas Heinkel was developing a genuine single seat fighter, the He 100, the Me 209 was designed from the start as a record breaking aircraft aimed at gaining the absolute speed record. It later transpired that Heinkel's design could easily have gone into series production as a single seat fighter after some slight modifications, whereas the Me 209 was totally unsuitable as a fighter aircraft, even after modifications. Both the He 100 and the Me 209 used a complicated system of surface radiators to reduce drag. One of Heinkel's employees had developed the explosive rivet and these were used for the first time on the He 100 with resulting savings in the cost of construction. Heinkel and Messerschmitt went ahead with development at their own risk. Both constructed three test aircraft initially. Later Heinkel built nine more test aircraft. Messerschmitt first built two and one more much later. The fifth test aircraft was to be a completely new design.

The Heinkel factory was quickest: the He 100 V1 took off for its maiden flight on 22 January 1938 and was transferred to Rechlin on 1 April 1938 on satisfactory completion of the works test flying programme. The second He 100, the V2, D-IUOS, was to be used for an attack on the world record and was completed at the end of May 1938. At this stage the Me 209 V1 was still being built. On Whit Monday, 5 June 1938, Udet turned up at Rostock. The He 100 V2 was at the Marienehe Works airfield and the record was to be attempted in the next few days by Flugkapitän Herting. Udet, who had already flown the He 100 V1 at Rechlin, now wanted to fly the V2. He just wanted to try it. It turned out to be a record breaking flight which would be officially recognised, as official FAI observers were present. Udet took off in the He 100 V2 at 16.27, crossed the start line at Müritz, roared off towards Wustrow and was back in Müritz 9 minutes 27.4 seconds later. He landed at Rostock-Marienehe at 16.53. He had beaten the Italian-held world record for land based aircraft over 100 km by 50mph with an average speed of 393.9mph! Udet was impressed with the performance of the aircraft but evasive about possible series production.

In September 1938 the clipped wing He 100 V3 was to make an attempt on the absolute world speed record. It crashed. He 100 V4, V5, V6 and V7 were built and transferred to Rechlin.

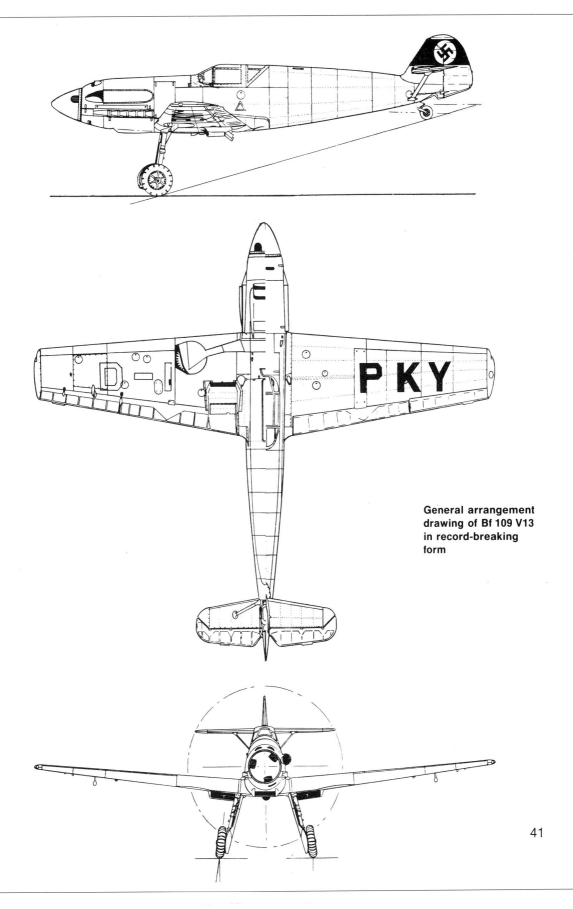

General arrangement
drawing of Bf 109 V13
in record-breaking
form

41

Me 209 V1, D-INJR, was completed in the Summer of 1938. The Messerschmitt chief test pilot, Dr Wurster, was at the controls for its maiden flight on 1 August 1938. The aircraft used the same engine as the He 100 V2, namely the DB 601 A, but it had some very unpleasant handling characteristics. The evaporative cooling system did not work properly either. Heinkel had also encountered this problem. Two further test aircraft, Me 209 V2, D-IWAH, and V3, D-IVFP, were built and all three subjected to an intensive test flying programme. There were twenty test flights altogether. Whereas the He 100 test aircraft presented few problems apart from cooling difficulties, it was demonstrated time and time again that the Me 209 was unfit for service use. Heinkel and Messerschmitt worked desperately to prepare an aircraft for the attack on the world record, in the meantime the development of the Bf 109 continued at Augsburg.

After the record flight Bf 109 V13 became V15, D-IPHR (E-03), the prototype for the E series. The development of the E series was not without its problems, so further test aircraft had to be built. They were Bf 109 V16, D-IPGS (E-04), V17, D-IWKU (E-05), and V18, D-ITXP (E-06). The main problem encountered in developing the E series was the whole question of wing-mounted weapons. To solve these problems there was intensive co-operation between Messerschmitt and the Luftwaffe weapon testing centre at Tarnewitz. All sorts of weapon combinations were tried and finally it was decided to equip the E-1 series with two MG 17s above the engine and two MG 17s in the wings. Series production started at the end of 1938; reaching full scale in 1939. Apart from Messerschmitt (previously BFW) Regensburg, other firms were now brought into the production process, namely AGO, Arado, Erla, Fieseler, Focke-Wulf, and Wiener-Neustädter Flugzeugwerke (WNF).

They were successful in overcoming the difficulties associated with wing mounted cannons (MG/FF) so that the Bf 109 E-1 was soon available for service armed with two MG/FFs and two MG 17s. Approximately 40 of the E1 series went to Legion Condor in Spain during the final phase of the Spanish Civil War and established the superiority of the Bf 109. During 1939 the Luftwaffe JGs were converted one by one to the series E version.

There were some striking changes in the E series including the division of the cooling system into three sections: the oil cooler on the underside of the nose and the two engine radiators inboard on the underside of the wings immediately next to the fuselage. Just in front of the firewall on the port side was the air intake for the supercharger and this took the form of a venetian blind-type duct.

So far the engines had all powered two-bladed propellers but the DB 601 in the E series had electric variable pitch three-bladed VDM propellers. The oil reservoir was immediately behind the firewall, the fuel tank under and behind the pilot's seat. Between the seat and the fuel tank there was 8mm thick steel armour plate which extended above the pilot's head. The radio equipment (transmitter and receiver) was housed in the middle of the fuselage between the cockpit and the tail. The undercarriage consisted of cantilever sprung legs which retracted outwards hydraulically. An oxygen system was included as the E series, although flown at heights up to 29,500 ft, did not have a pressurised cockpit.

In the meantime the Third Reich propaganda machine went from strength to

Heinkel He 100 V2 after Udet's record-breaking flight on 6 June 1938. Standing in front of the aircraft from left to right: "Jupp" Köhler, Schwärzler, Siegfried Günter, Udet, Heinkel, Hertel, Herting

Bf 109 V15 (E-03) D-IPHR

Above: Bf 109 V16 (E-04) with a typical Bf 109 undercarriage failure. Below: Bf 109 V17 was completely written off in an emergency field landing

Above: Completed Bf 109 E-1s. In the foreground an aircraft for Switzerland. A surprisingly large number of Bf 109s with civilian registration marks. Below: The first series-built Bf 109 E-1 is rolled out of the final assembly hangar

Condor Legion: Above left:
J 88 before a mission.
Above right: Hauptmann Handrick,
head of J 88. Below: Living
quarters of 2. Staffel

Bf 109 E-1 of J 88 (above). Right: The fin of Werner Mölders' Bf 109 after 15 kills. Below: Bf 109 E-1 of 2/J 88 with He 111E of K 88

strength. Charles Lindbergh, famous for his solo crossing of the Atlantic, had been invited by Udet to visit the Luftwaffe. He was so impressed that he told anybody who was interested that the German Luftwaffe had such first rate aircraft that it was unbeatable. The Commander in Chief of the French Air Force, General Vuillemin, was given the opportunity to observe the Bf 109 E in flight. In June 1938 Udet had invited his American friend Major Williams to Germany. During that visit there was a rather one-sided swop: Udet flew the Curtis Gulfhawk and Williams flew a Bf 109. Every newspaper in America carried Williams' report on his flight in the Bf 109 on 15 June 1938. He wrote: "Today I flew the Messerschmitt 109, the latest single seat German fighter aircraft . . . and I am the only person to have flown it – apart from German Luftwaffe pilots. I think I was allowed to do so because they wanted to hear the opinion of an objective observer . . . My whole life has been devoted to the development of fighter aircraft and especially fighter aircraft with fixed guns – so that you aim with the whole aircraft . . . I do know the maximum speed of the Me 109 but I have been sworn to secrecy. I must say, however, that I was very surprised at its low landing speed and that I regard the Me 109 as the fastest single seat production fighter in the world.

It really does offer the best compromise between maximum speed, manoeuvrability and low landing speed of any aircraft I have ever flown. It responds to the slightest movement of the joystick and after a practice landing and a few minutes in the air I felt totally at home in the Me 109 . . . It's a pilot's plane, what every fighter pilot dreams of . . . I didn't imagine it . . . I am simply telling you about what in my opinion is the most manoeuvrable single seat fighter

in the world . . . I have seen a number of English single seat fighters such as the Hawker Hurricane, and the Spitfire . . . but I would go for the Me 109 any day." Reports like this made people believe that the German Luftwaffe really was unbeatable and that it was necessary to produce something even better. In Germany the idea was fostered that only the Me 109 should be built as a standard fighter. In whose interest that was has never been completely established.

To emphasise the superiority of the Me 109 (as the Bf 109 was now generally known) and to emphasise the need for large scale series production of this one German fighter type, both at home and abroad, a deception was engineered in 1939 and to this day nobody knows who was responsible for it. On 30 May 1939 Hans Dieterle, the 23 year old Heinkel test pilot, flew the He 100 V8, D-IDGH, which had a DB 601 tuned to produce 1800 PS. He flew the prescribed measured distance at a maximum speed of 463.6mph and so beat the absolute world air speed record. It is worth mentioning that the airframe was identical to that of a series fighter and that only the engine had been tuned.

Soon afterwards on 26 April 1939 Fritz Wendel, the Messerschmitt pilot, flew the Me 209 V1 with an identical engine at a speed of 468.9mph and regained the world record from Heinkel. The deception was that the aircraft was identified to the FAI as a Bf 109 R and the entry in the record book is still shown as such. This made people think that the record speed had been flown with a special version of the Bf 109 single-seater fighter, but that was incorrect as the Me 209 was a totally different aircraft.

This deception was maintained consistently as we see from the example of the

Left: Messerschmitt with a French officer from General Vuillemin's entourage. Below, left: (l. to r.) Croneiss, Hentzen, Amann, Hitler, Udet, Messerschmitt. Below, right: Messerschmitt with Rudolf Hess, his patron

A posed propaganda photo: Köhler lifts Dieterle. The aircraft in the background is a normal He 100 D-0 with stuck on markings (!). Below is the actual He 100 V-8 used to break the world record

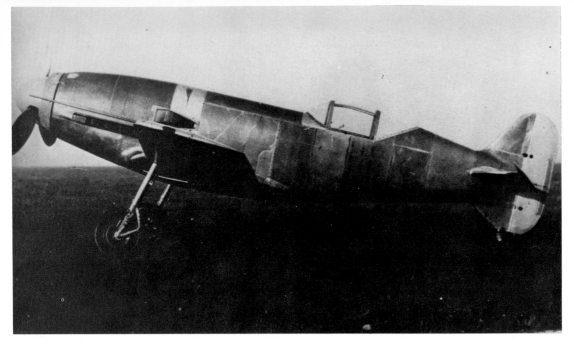

Right: Bf 109 E-1 on ➤
manoeuvres in 1939

The Me 209 V1 looked
like this at the time of
the record flight

Another posed propaganda photo:
Messerschmitt congratulates Wendel

Messerschmitt Bf 109 E with spinner removed

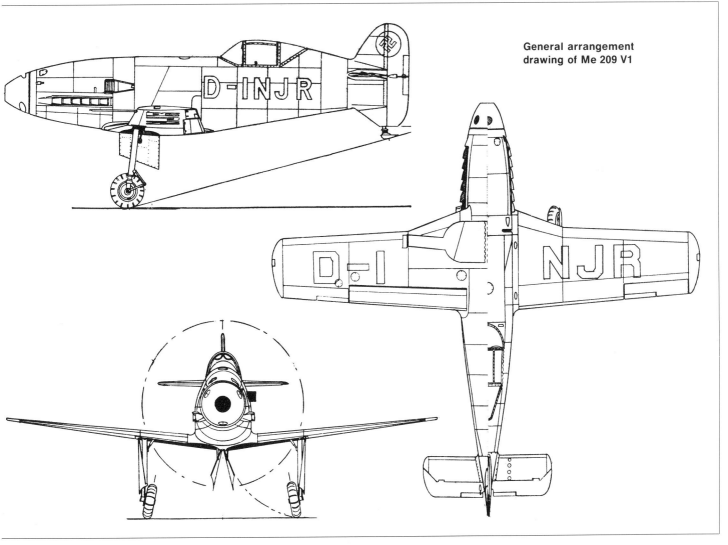

General arrangement drawing of Me 209 V1

aviation writer Rolf Italiaan who was well known at the time and as late as 1941 wrote in his book 'Wegbereiter deutscher Luftgeltung': "The Me 109 record is particularly worthy as it was flown with a series production German fighter." The German fighter pilots who were flying the 109 at the Front knew very well that no 109 could ever achieve 469mph – even with a tail wind!

A further point was that the Me 209 record had been flown under more favourable air pressure conditions. Heinkel now wanted to prove that when flown under the same air pressure conditions the He 100 was superior and so he intended to make another attempt on the record. But the RLM did not want Heinkel to build a fighter in competition with Messerschmitt. On 12 July 1939 General-Ingenieur Lucht, Udet's right hand man, informed Heinkel that the RLM was not interested in a fresh attempt on the record. The Bf 109 had finally come out on top. England, France, Italy and all other countries were building at least two fighter designs parallel to each other but in Germany there had now been a clear decision to build only one type of fighter aircraft. The lack of wisdom in this decision became apparent in 1940. The Bf 109 had finally become the standard fighter in the Luftwaffe and that was what it remained through to the end of the war, because Tank's Fw 190 was later used as a fighter bomber and ground attack aircraft rather than as a fighter.

2. Blitzkrieg and Sitzkrieg

The propaganda presentation of the Bf 109 as a superior fighter was backed up by speed records established by other German aircraft. These propaganda coups always had the same intention, namely to further Hitler's political aims. The annexation of Czechoslovakia and its transformation into the so-called Protectorate of Bohemia and Moravia, produced violent reactions in England, France and the United States, but no direct counter-measures. Hitler also wanted to resolve the "Polish question" as he called it. The records set up by the He 100 and the Me 209 were very timely for this. As a final warning to the West not to get militarily involved, Hitler's birthday on 20 April 1939 was celebrated by a military parade in Berlin which totally outshone all previous ones. Hitler hoped that this show of military strength would be sufficient to prevent England and France getting involved – but this time his bluff failed . . .

In the meantime the Bf 109 E-1 had become the standard Luftwaffe fighter. It had a maximum speed of 329mph, climbed at 3000ft per minute, with a ceiling of 36,000ft. But already a problem had become apparent which by 1940 would prove that this fighter was badly designed. The range of the Bf 109 B-2 was 465 miles but now the E-1 had a range of only 410 miles. There was no room in the small lightweight airframe for the larger fuel tanks necessary for the more powerful engine and yet even at the design state it had been known that the 700PS engines would soon be replaced by more powerful ones. The Bf 109 E had other shortcomings too. The B and D series aircraft had already shown a tendency to ground-loop on take-off and landing and in the E series this tendency was accentuated. Peacetime training of young fighter pilots in 1939 had been thorough and conscientious, but it could not prevent more than 1500 Bf 109 Es ground-looping and being wrecked at take-off or landing, either during training or on active service.

But in spite of these well-known weaknesses, there was interest abroad in the Bf 109 because of the carefully targeted propaganda. Yugoslavia ordered 73 Bf 109 Es, Rumania 69, Switzerland 80, the recently-founded Slovakia 16 and Hungary 40. In addition Hungary built the 109 under licence at a factory in Gyer. In the context of the Non-aggression Pact between the Soviet Union and the German Reich, five Bf 109 Es went to Russia. Japan ordered two Bf 109 Es. It has often been claimed that the Japanese fighter, the Kawasaki Ki61 "Hien" (swallow), which was very similar to the Bf 109, had been developed from it. However this is factually incorrect as the first Ki 61 had been produced in Japan six

◄ Opposite Top: Bf 109E
destined for Slovakia

Centre: Export Bf 109
for Switzerland

Bottom: This Bf 109 E
was sold to Russia

Top: Bf 109 E of Furio
Niclot, the successful
Italian fighter pilot

Centre: Yugoslavia
purchased 73
Bf 109 Es

Bottom: Bf 109 E in
Japan

months before the arrival of the first Bf 109 E.

In the meantime development work went ahead on the Bf 109. An ETC bomb release was fitted to a small number of Bf 109 E-1s, so producing the first fighter bomber. The Bf 109 E-1B could carry an SC 250 bomb.

About then two of the E-0 series aircraft, E-07 and E-08 became Bf 109 V19 and V20 (D-IRRT & CE + BM) and were used for work on the new E-3 and E-2 versions. V20 seems to have been the only example of the E-2 series but V19 became the prototype for the E-3 which went into large scale production. When war broke out thirteen Luftwaffe fighter groups were equipped with Bf 109 E and D versions. There were only isolated cases of Bf 109 Bs and Cs being used at the front as most had been transferred to fighter pilot training establishments. According to returns by the Luftwaffe Quartermaster General dated September 2 1939 there were 389 Bf 109 Ds and 667 Bf 109 Es in the Luftwaffe fighter and heavy fighter formations of which 348 and 598 respectively were serviceable. It is worth noting in this context that at this time production numbers of the Bf 110 had been inadequate for the needs of the heavy fighter wings as 277 (259) Bf 109 Ds and 36 (36) Bf 109 Es of the aircraft mentioned above were with heavy fighter units. Bf 109 Ds were flying with I./ZG 2, Stab and I, II. and III./ZG 26, II./ZG 52 and II./ZG 76. The 36 Bf 109 Es were all with II.ZG 1.

The invasion of Poland began on September 1 – and that signalled the start of World War II. German fighter pilots soon encountered little resistance in Poland so the Bf 109 really only had a role at the start. The invasion of Poland mainly relied on bombers, dive bombers and heavy fighters.

The Technisches Amt was set up in the RLM and new aircraft projects were incorporated in the so-called G/LC list. Aircraft manufacturers were allocated blocks from the sequential numbers on the list with the manufacturer's abbreviation as a prefix. All new Messerschmitt types developed between the birth of the RLM and July 1 1938 had the prefix 'Bf' (Bayrische Flugzeugwerke AG) and from that date onwards 'Me', denoting the change to Messerschmitt AG. The Bf 108, Bf 109 and Bf 110 belong to the former category and were never renamed.

During the war years however it became normal practice in the press, on radio and in general conversation to refer to the 'Me 109' and 'Me 110'. In aeronautical engineering circles and in official service use (at least in the higher echelons) the technically correct designation was always used.

Both forms have been used in this book. The strictly correct term is used with reference to the various series produced versions but where the reference to the 109 is more general the colloquial term 'Me 109' is used.

General arrangement drawing of Bf 109 E ➤

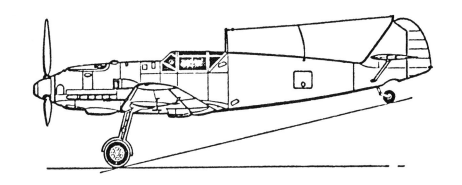

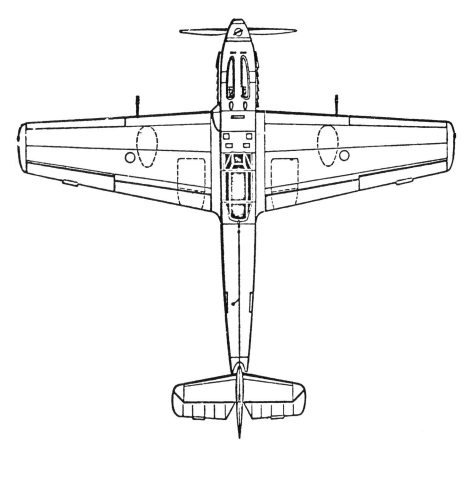

59

Aircraft Briefing Document   Types Bf 109 E-1 and E-3
Luftwaffe Head of Training 7.7.1939

Berlin, 7 July 1939

Reichsminister of the Air Ministry
and Commander in Chief of the Luftwaffe
Head of Air Training
Abt.St.A.Luftw.
Az: 67 a/8 No 803/39 geh (IA 1)
Re: Genst. 1. Abt No 842/39 (II,3) dated 14.6.1939
Re: Bf 109 E
Briefing Document on Aircraft Types Bf 109 E-1 and E-3

1.	Designation:	Bayrische Flugzeugwerke 109 E-1
		Bayrische Flugzeugwerke 109 E-3
2.	Abbreviated Designation:	Bf 109 E-1
		Bf 109 E-3
3.	Classification of Equipment:	8. Airframes
4.	Equipment Category:	F1
5.	Order Code:	F1-
6.	Role:	Fighter aircraft
7.	Crew:	1 pilot
8.	Equipment:	
	category 1:	for Bf 109 E-1
		2 synchronised MG 17s, 2 x 1000 rounds
		2 wing mounted MG 17s with 2 x 500 rounds
		1 ESK 2000 (for practice)
		for Bf 109 E-3
		2 synchronised MG 17s with 2 x 1000 rounds
		2 wing mounted MGFFs with 2 x 60 rounds
		1 ESK 2000 (for practice)
	category 9:	DB 601A
	category 10:	seat parachute
	category 24 a-d:	FuG VII radio
		1 flare pistol and 5 rounds
9.	Allocation:	In accordance with the current tables of equipment laid down in the authorised strength of fighter aircraft
10:	Manufacturer's documentation:	Equipment no: 8-109
		Version E-1
		Version E-3
11:	Equipment description:	Aircraft manual: Bf 109 E-1
		Bf 109 E-3 or
		Abbreviated
		manual: Bf 109 E-1
		Bf 109 E-3
12:	Weight:	Max. All Up Weight: 2585 kg
13:	Comments:	Brief cloud flying permitted

per pro
v. der Osten
F.d.R.
signature

Bf 109 V 19 (E-07)

61

Above: V 20 (E-08) works no. 5601, CE + BM, seems to
be the only example of the Bf 109 E-2 series

Opposite: Top left: Series
manufacture of Bf 109 E. Right:
Fitting the wing. Below:
Completing final details in the
Bf 109 cockpit. Right: Mounting the
wing guns

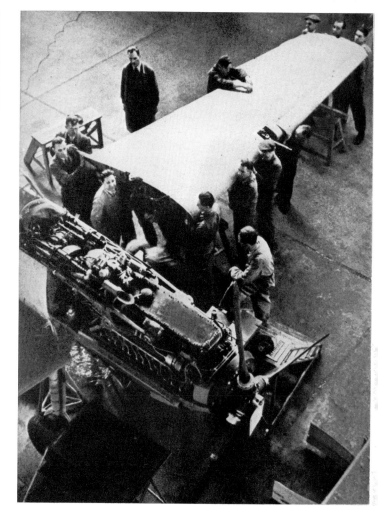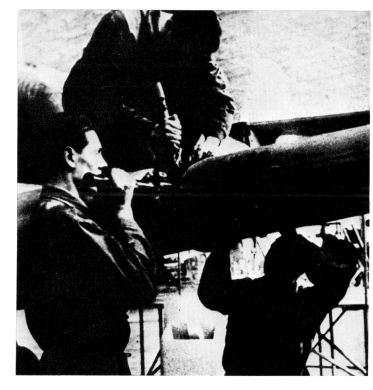

Bf 109 E-3 of 2./JG 20
is armed

Bf 109 E-3 scramble -
1. Staffel of JG 20

Bf 109 E-3 of
JG 53

Bf 109 E-1 of
6/JG 26 on
manoeuvres,
10 August
1939

Bf 109 E-3 of
Zestör-
ergeschwader
1 after
crashing with
a collapsed
undercarriage
at
Prague-Rusin

Above: Fuelling a Bf 109 E. Below: the first mechanic closes the canopy of the Bf 109 E-3. The squadron emblem is clearly visible

The formations used in the invasion of Poland were:

Luftflotte 1 (Gen. d. Fl. Kesselring)

I./(J)LG 2	Hptm. Trübenbach	Bf 109 E	Operational base:	Malzkow, Lettin
II./ZG 1	Maj. Reichardt	Bf 109 E	Operational base:	Mühlen
I./JG 76	Maj. Woldenga	Bf 109 E	Operational base:	Arys/Rostken
I./JG 77	Maj. Mettig	Bf 109 D	Operational base:	Jesau

Luftflotte 4 (Genlt. Löhr)

I./ZG 2	Hptm. Gentzen	Bf 109 D	Operation base:	Groß-Stein/Oppeln

It had been assumed that the invasion of Poland would provoke Polish air retaliation against Berlin, Königsberg, Stettin, Breslau or other towns in the Reich, so 24 fighter squadrons equipped with the Bf 109 E were reserved for defence of the German Reich:

Stab JG 2	Obst. von Massow	Operational base:	Döberitz
I./JG 2	Maj. Viek	Operational base:	Döberitz (excl. 1 St)
I./JG 20	Hptm. Lützow	Operational base:	Sprottau, Döberitz, Straußberg
10./JG 2	Hptm. Blumensaat	Operational base:	Fürstenwalde
4./JG 2	Maj. Burgaller	Operational base:	Döberitz
Stab JG 3	Obstlt. Ibel	Operational base:	Bernburg
I./JG 3	?	Operational base:	Brandis nr. Leipzig
I./JG 76	Hptm. Müller-Rienzburg	Operational base:	Stubendorf
I./JG 77	Hptm. Janke	Operational base:	Oels
Fighter Pilot Training School 1	Oberst Osterkamp	Operational base:	Werneuchen

(The Fighter Pilot Training School flew Bf 109 C and E)

Although no Polish air attacks ensued, only I./JG 76 and I./JG 77 were deployed over Poland. The superiority of the Luftwaffe over Poland both in terms of numbers and performance proved overwhelming. 1,600 modern aircraft were lined up against approximately 1,170 Polish aircraft of which only about 400 at most could be regarded as being modern. The Messerschmitts soon gained control of the air. They were generally used to escort bombers and dive-bombers, and to provide low level attack support for the army. It was these low level attacks which cost the majority of fighter losses as the Polish anti-aircraft defences were very effective. A total of 67 Bf 109s were lost over Poland. Just eight days after the beginning of hostilities, the first of the fighter units were withdrawn from the East and returned to Germany. The most successful fighter pilot in the Polish campaign was the Kommandeur of I./ZG 2, Hauptmann Gentzen who achieved seven kills flying a Bf 109 D-1.

In the closing months of 1939 major series production of Me 109 E-3 started, though they were only delivered from the beginning of January 1940. Through to the end of 1939 only Bf 109 D-1s and E-1s saw front line service. The Bf 109 E-3 was outwardly very similar to the E-1, although front line experience had led to structural changes to strengthen the airframe. For example the cabin fairing frame was reinforced and extra armour plating added to the pilot's seat. The armament was increased by installing a MG/FFM motor cannon in addition to three MG/FFs and two MG 17s. This made the E-3 the most heavily armed series production single-seat fighter in the world. It was more heavily armed than even the Hurricane or the Spitfire because their eight 7.62mm machine guns could not match the fire power of the three 20mm cannon. Whereas the D-1 had an all-up weight of 2420kg the weight of the E-3 had increased to 2600kg.

During the Polish campaign the Germans had to take into account the possibility of attack from the West. Accordingly the following units had remained there:

Stab, I and II./JG 26	Bf 109 E
I./JG 52	Bf 109 D
Stab, I and II./ZG 26	Bf 109 B & D
II./JG 77	Bf 109 E
II./JG 188	Bf 109 D
J. Gr. 126 (became III./ZG 26)	Bf 109 D
II. Staffel LG 2	Bf 109 B,E
Stab and II./JG 52	Bf 109 E
I./JG 51	Bf 109 E
10 Staffel JG 72	Bf 109 E
Stab, I and II./JG 53	Bf 109 E
J. Gr. 152 (became I./ZG 52)	Bf 109 D
I./JG 54	Bf 109 E
J. Gr. 176 (became II./ZG 76)	Bf 109 D
I./JG 71	Bf 109 E
Stab JG 77	Bf 109 E

By the end of 1939 there had been no major fighter engagements on the Western Front nor had the other formations seen real service. As neither French nor Germans took the inititiave the period up to the start of the German offensive in the West in the spring of 1940 was known as the Sitzkrieg (Phoney War). Any military engagements in the West up to then had consisted of short range and long range reconnaissance aircraft from both sides making sorties, almost always with fighter escort. The escort fighters usually went into the attack. As the English had sent an expeditionary force to France the Bf 109s met not only

French but also English aircraft. The English mostly flew the Bristol Blenheim as their reconnaissance aircraft and the Hawker Hurricane as escort fighter. The French had the Potez 63 as their reconnaissance aircraft, though sometimes, much less often, the Bloch 131 and Bloch 200. Short range reconnaissance was generally covered by the single engined Mureaux. The French tended to use the Morane 406 C.1 and the Curtiss H.75 (imported from the USA) as their fighter escorts.

Otherwise both sides sat tight and prepared for the next offensive. It had become apparent that no satisfactory solution had been found to major problems such as fighter escort, compatibility of weapons, communications and air raid warning services. There was now time to perfect the training and to carry out major manoeuvres and exercises. Intermittent sorties by the French and English had demonstrated that German air defence had considerable weaknesses in important respects. One especially weak point was air observation, although there was a close network of observation posts in all areas, staffed with volunteers and reservists, ready to carry out their task with great enthusiasm and even more idealism. Unfortunately they were just short of the necessary equipment and expertise. Their reports based on optical and acoustic observation were passed on using rudimentary telecommunications.

These observation posts were called Flugwachen and were organised in so-called Flugwachkommandos. There the messages were assessed and then passed on to the flight information centre of the appropriate Luftgaukommando in a simple form. The flight information centre compiled all the messages from the Flugwachkommandos (Flukos) in its region and produced an air situation report which formed the basis on which fighter aircraft and flak were deployed. This information was passed on to the Luftflotten (air fleets). Needless to say there were numerous weak links in this system. In particular it was difficult to obtain a clear picture of the overall current situation from the plethora of individual reports. And yet such an overview was necessary if the fighters were to be deployed at the right moment. The fighter formations were at their bases in a state of readiness, the highest level of alert being known as "Sitzbereitschaft". With this alert the aircraft were supposed to be ready to take off within three minutes. There was a telephone link between the operational

French soldiers investigate the wreckage of a Bf 109 E shot down over French territory

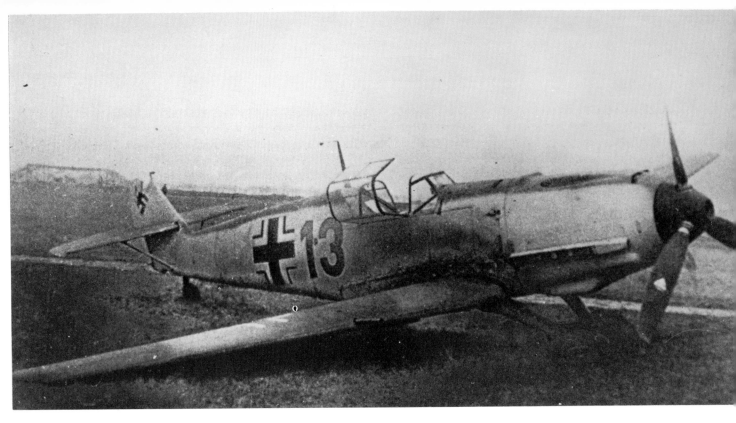

Crash landing of a Bf 109 E-3 of JG 2 at Döberitz-Elsgrund

Bf 109 E-1 of 11./JG 54 showing the wing emblem: "Lion of Aspern"

headquarters of the fighter formation and the Luftgau and the nearest Fluko. After take-off the air situation was transmitted to the formation leader by radio. At that stage of the war there was still no direction-finding system for position fixing. The fighters still depended on good weather and being able to see the ground.

The formation leaders reported their experiences of contact with enemy fighters but they also commented on the behaviour of the Bf 109 on the ground. Provided the ground on the airfield was frozen they had no particular problems with the aircraft apart from the occasional ground-loop on take-off or landing. But when the ground was soft the 109 soon demonstrated that its undercarriage could not cope with such conditions. There was unanimous agreement that in the air it was superior to all enemy fighters. Being less streamlined, the Morane and the Curtiss had no chance except in tight manoeuvres in dogfights. The 109 could easily out-manoeuvre the Hurricane Mk.1A.

Then the Luftwaffe received their first "Freya" radar location equipment. One of these devices was in the Trier area, one on the island of Wangerooge, a further installation was set up in December 1939 at Landstuhl in the Palatinate. Early in 1940 further installations followed in Kandel, Aachen (Aix-la-Chapelle), Kleve, Vilsum and Stadtkyll. Using the installation at Trier it was already possible to direct fighter operations on the French frontier to some extent. The installation on Wangerooge was to play a special role. On 18 December 1939 it was instrumental in enabling German fighters and heavy fighters to catastrophically defeat an offensive British bomber formation through early recognition of their approach. What actually happened over the German Bight has never quite been ascertained because German reports of losses were much higher than the British ones. The British maintained that only 24 Vickers Wellingtons were involved. Eye-witnesses still alive today counted up to 44 Wellingtons in a clear sky! The British still maintain there were only 22 aircraft of which ten returned home. So the number returning may be assumed to be ten. But the German report at that time mentions 56 attacking aircraft, which would mean that 46 Wellingtons had been shot down.

Eyewitness accounts clearly confirm 32 kills. On the German side two Bf 109s were shot down. The leader of the German formations in this first air battle in the Second World War was Oberstleutnant Schumacher, Kommodore of JG 1. It is worth mentioning that Leutnant Steinhoff, leader of 10./JG 26 and later to become Inspekteur der Luftwaffe der Bundeswehr, was the first to reach the English formation and succeeded in shooting down two aircraft. Oberstleutnant Schumacher was appointed "Jagdfliegerführer (Jafü) Deutsche Bucht".

As the Bf 109 E-3 was supplied during the Spring of 1940 it was allocated to fighter formations one after the other. Operation "Weserübung", the occupation of Norway and Denmark, increased the war in the air. As a German attack was expected in the West, the French and the English Air Forces increased their efforts with short range and long range reconnaissance to discover the secret of the timing of the German attack. This meant that in the West there were repeated clashes between air defence and escort fighters of both sides. Also the RAF began harassment raids using small formations of bombers. As the English Wellingtons, Hampdens and Blenheims were usually intercepted by German

The "Jafü German Bight" Major Schumacher at JG 1 in Jever, 1939, with his Adjutant

Bf 109 E-1 of JG 1 ditched on the beach at Langeoog

Oberstleutnant Schumacher shortly before taking-off to do battle (German Bight)

Bf 109 E-1s going in to attack

Winter of 1939/49: Bf 109 E-3 of II./JG 77 in Nordholz. Maintaining the aircraft was not pleasant in the depths of Winter

II./JG 77 at Nordholz, Winter 1939/40: some of the aircraft still have the old 70/71/65 colours, others the new 71/02/65

Above and below: After the ''Weserübung'' II./JG 77 were in Christiansand. This is the Bf 109 E-3 flown by Commander Major Harry von Bülow-Bothkamp with Oberfeldwebel Jordan and Oberfeldwebel Hamann and a fitter

Opposite: Visit by Generaloberst Milch (second from right) to II./JG 77 at Varnes-Drontheim May 1940

Centre: Bf 109 C-2 of II./JG 2 at Varnes, 1940

Bottom: The same aircraft at Stavanger 1942, where they were to be used as night fighters

fighters they often attempted to escape via Switzerland. But the Swiss were determined to maintain strict neutrality and shot down any aircraft that strayed over their frontiers. Often German fighters or heavy fighters would cross the frontier in hot pursuit and so it came about that Swiss Bf 109s would shoot down German Bf 110s or other German aircraft.

It was not until the beginning of the German offensive in the West that the German fighter pilots were relieved of the stress of the 'Sitzkrieg'. The campaign in France, Belgium and Holland was to be a story of triumph for the Messerschmitt 109 E-3.

It was at this time that Messerschmitt tried again to make a fighter out of the Me 209. A new prototype Me 209 V4 was started. It was registered as D-IRND, but then changed to CE+BW. The Me 209 V4 had a new increased span wing and also slots. The fuselage was exactly the same as for the first three test aircraft. It was armed with an MK 108 (30mm calibre) motor cannon and two MG 17s in the wing roots. Attempts to install two MK 108s in the outer wing were unsuccessful as the airfoil section of the wing was too slim to accommodate the ammunititon feed and the pipework to the evaporative cooling system. The test flights were not exactly encouraging: the cooling system was inadequate, the controls were too heavy and the aircraft was unstable in roll. Change after change was made in an attempt to produce a satisfactory result. It was all in vain. When the aircraft was transferred to Rechlin the test pilots there confirmed that this aircraft was much too complicated for pilots with normal training and was absolutely useless for military use on front line airfields.

Incidentally the He 100, which the RLM had declined, was approved for export after Heinkel had abandoned the evaporative cooling system and replaced it with normal radiators. Japan and Russia bought some of these aircraft. Powered by the DB601 Aa, they achieved a maximum speed of almost 435mph without armament, and produced no particular handling problems. Taxiing was straightforward. The Me 209 was only to be resurrected again in 1942/43 because then the RLM put a stop to the development of new projects.

In the campaign in the West, German fighter pilots knew from the start that it would be a hard battle, although the strength of the French Air Force had been considerably underestimated. It was thought that there were only about 150 Morane 406, 60 Curtiss H.75 and 40 Dewoitine D 520. In fact there were 1070 Morane 406, 266 Curtiss H.75 and 65 Dewoitine 520, in addition to which there were almost 500 Bloch 151, 152 and 155. Although only the Bloch and the Dewoitine could really be classified as high performance fighters the Morane squadrons were always flown with spirit. The problem for the French was that although they had 1936 fighter aircraft a large number of them were in depots and in pilot training schools so that the actual number available for use was only approximately 750 fighter aircraft. The total picture looked like this:

Holland	200 aircraft
Belgium	400 aircraft
England	900 aircraft
France	3400 aircraft
Total approx.	4900 aircraft

On the other side Luftlotten 2 and 3 could muster only about 3800 aircraft of all types. However, whereas all the aircraft in the German Luftwaffe were modern, a large

When the Me 209 V4 was presented to the public as a new fighter it carried this imaginative decoration

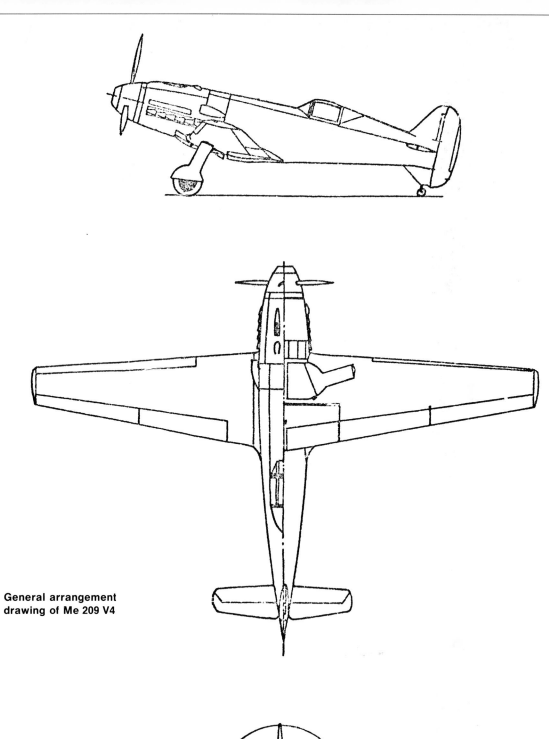

**General arrangement
drawing of Me 209 V4**

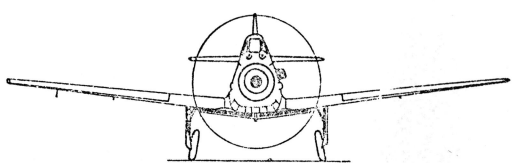

80

proportion of the Dutch, Belgian and French aircraft were obsolete. The inferiority of the British Hurricane (the Spitfire was not yet in active service) to the Bf 109 E-3 had already become apparent during the 'Sitzkrieg'.

On the German side the only Bf 109 formations available in the German Bight area were Stab JG 1, I and II./JG186. I.(J)/LG2 in reserve. The Jafü of Luftflotte 2 had thirteen fighter wings with four group staff available, the Jafü of Loftflotte 3 fourteen fighter wings with five group staffs. The heavy fighter formations have not been included here as they had transferred almost completely to the Bf 110 by this time. The Luftwaffe had 1260 Bf 109 fighters of which 1016 were fully operational. An entry from the daily log of JG27 dated 10 May 1940 shows how intensive the sorties were:

| Aircraft | 101 |
| Sorties flown | 326 |

That means that each pilot in the squadron must have flown at least three sorties in one day and many of them even four.

During these hostilities a problem arose that was later to have serious implications for fighter pilots during the Battle of Britain. The British fighters avoided the German fighters and in small groups attacked the Stukas and ground attack aircraft which suffered serious losses. So it was not without reason that direct fighter protection was demanded. However the head of VIII Fliegerkorps, Generalleutnant von Richthofen, rejected this idea, "because tying the fighters closely to battle formations was contrary to the very essence of the Luftwaffe and it was impractical to combine the high speed of fighters with the slower Stukas and bombers".

The German combat and Stuka formations carried out a surprise attack early on the morning of 10 May 1940 and virtually eliminated the Dutch and the Belgian Air Forces at a stroke. From the second day of the offensive fighter aircraft found virtually no opposition in this area with the result that they could be used for low-level attack to support the army.

The degree of superiority of the Bf 109 over Belgian and Dutch aircraft is seen from a report by Adolf Galland, who was at that time Hauptmann Galland: "I was lucky. My first kill was easy. I almost had a bad conscience about it. The Belgians were flying obsolete Hurricanes (Mk.1) and even experienced pilots would have had little chance against our Me 109 Es. Our aircraft were vastly superior to them in speed, rate of climb, armament and pilot experience."

But by 12 May things weren't looking so rosy. Fighter losses were increasing. For example JG 27 only had 85 of 101 aircraft serviceable on 10 May. It was at this time that the first Spitfires appeared. The Oberkommando of the Wehrmacht reported the destruction of 36 Spitfires on that day. In the meantime the French had noticed that the Bf 110 heavy fighter which had been regarded as very dangerous because of German propaganda was in fact fairly easy to shoot down. So together with other Bf 110 crews the Kommodore of ZG 76, Major Grabmann, was shot down by a Morane 406 on 15 May. He was taken prisoner but escaped and succeeded in getting back to the German lines. On 18 and 19 May there were serious air battles as the enemy was putting up a determined and courageous fight. These battles were connected with the advance of the von Kleist Panzergruppe which had pressed on far beyond St Quentin. Bf 109 E-3s reported that they had shot down 95 enemy aircraft on that day. But there is no doubt that the French gave a very

Bf 109 E-1s of III./JG 27 before the beginning of the French campaign in 1940. These aircraft still have the old 70/71/65 camouflage

One of the pilots in JG 2 ''Richthofen'' explains his cockpit instrumentation to members of the Waffen-SS

good account of themselves.

Werner Mölders (at that time Kommandeur of III./JG 53) discovered on 5 June 1940 how dangerous it was to rely on the superiority of the Me 109. He reported: "17.15 take-off, again with a squadron. We are flying to Amiens. The time is almost up. Aircraft above us. We cannot identify them. We climb to 23,000 ft. – only Me 109s. So we descend somewhat lower and gradually head for home. Then suddenly: six Moranes! I go into the attack, and in the middle of the attack I recognise two other Messerschmitt squadrons which are attacking the same aircraft from behind and above . . . They were on it first so I withdraw and watch from above. They shoot much too early, there is the usual dogfight and some of the Moranes fight valiantly. Then one Me 109 goes down in flames and the pilot floats down on his parachute. I watch this battle for a while and then I attack one Morane which three Me 109s have unsuccessfully engaged in a dogfight. Soon I have it in my sights – immediately it escapes again, but it hasn't had enough yet. Suddenly it climbs from below and I lose sight of it under my wing . . . then it's down below to one side. Damn! This Morane is still shooting too, though not very accurately. I peel off and climb into the sun. It must have lost me because it turns away in the opposite direction and disappears towards the south. Below two other Me 109s are still amusing themselves with one last Morane. I watch the dogfight which ends up at low level and the Morane proves a difficult target as it keeps turning sharply. A quick look behind and above – the sky is full of wheeling Me 109s. I am at about 2,600ft – then suddenly all hell is let loose in the cockpit and I feel ill. The throttle has been shot away, the joystick lurches forward and the ground is coming up to meet me. Out now or it's too late!"

Mölders parachuted safely but landed 37 miles behind French lines and was taken captive. He said about being shot down: "I can still see my aircraft diving out of control, the port wing badly damaged. Just before hitting the ground it zooms up again as if it can't believe that after 25 victories it has actually been beaten."

The French had discovered the vulnerability of the radiators on the Bf 109 and usually tried to hit these with the result that many Bf 109s were put out of action. For the British, supporting France was also gradually becoming a problem. The Hawker Hurricane was so inferior to the Bf 109 that British fighter squadron losses rose to a dangerous degree. Consequently the RAF decided to withdraw its fighter formations from France and from 20 May on only three squadrons remained. When these too were withdrawn it transpired that of the original 261 Hurricanes which had been in France on 10 May there only 66 were left to make the trip home across the Channel.

But despite this there was a definite crisis for the German fighter pilots. They had reached the limit of their capacity. Too much was being demanded of them – they were supposed to be everywhere at once. The von Kleist Panzergruppe reported for the first time on 24 May: "Enemy air superiority!" and General Guderian confirmed on 26 May: "Very strong enemy fighter activity. Our own fighter protection is totally inadequate!" But that was soon to change. The fighters were now called upon to escort the combat and Stuka formations closely. Escort protection was now more important than the number of kills. Success was rapid. Oberst Bülowius, the Kommandeur of I./LG 1 (LG = Lehrgeschwader – Training Group) a few days later: "Fighter protection was excellent

Opposite top: JG 2 in the west, 1940: Kommodore Oberstleutnant von Bülow (second from left) with Generaloberst Milch (left), General Loerzer (second from right) and Major Seegert at Bastogne. Bottom: Bülow prepares for a sortie. Temporary dark green camouflage on top of 71/02/65

France, 1940: Top and centre: Bf 109 Es of JG2; above: Staffelkapitän Hauptman von Winterfeld

One of the squadrons of JG 3 had a young lion as its mascot, here seen checking out the MG/FF of a Bf 109 E

85

The 71/02/65 camouflage proved to be too light, so in JG 2 the lighter parts were daubed dark green. Below: Major Lützow. Kommodore of JG 3 with Hauptmann Balthasar Kommandeur of III./JG 3 and his Bf 109 E-3 works no. 1559

Top: Major Mix,
Kommandeur of
III./JG 2 with the
Bf 109 E in which he
was shot down over
France. Centre:
Bf 109 E of 6. Staffel
JG 26 shot down on
June 1 1940. Bottom:
Bf 109 E-3 of I./JG 3
shot down over
France

and were able to drop bombs just as if we were on the practice range.''

Here for the first time German fighter pilots learnt what fighter escort duties really meant and this was experience which they bitterly needed later on in the Battle of Britain.

On 26 and 27 May there were violent air battles round Calais, Lille, Amiens and Dunkirk. The British were evacuating their Expeditionary Force. To protect the evacuation the British had brought in stronger Spitfire formations, with the result that the German fighters suffered heavy losses over Dunkirk. Poor weather affected the activities of the German fighters whose airfields near the front had turned into mudbaths. At the end of May the Germans thought that they detected a reduction in British fighter activity. One fighter group reported for example: ''Enemy fighters were easily driven off. We did not manage to shoot any down!'' Another report read: ''It has often been our experience that complete Spitfire squadrons turn tail as soon as they recognise the Bf 109 homing in on them. Twice they attempted to approach the bombers. When the Bf 109s intercepted they turned tail.'' What they didn't realise was that the British were preserving their fighter aircraft as they expected a German invasion of Britain. How wise they were was shown a few weeks later. On 4 June Dunkirk fell.

Operation ''Paula'' was the beginning of the final battle for France, a major attack on the airfields, depots and arms factories around Paris and three Fliegerkorps with all their formations took part. Command of the fighter formations was in the hands of Jafü 3, Oberst von Massow. Although the French had already suffered heavy losses they could still be dangerous as was discovered by some squadron leaders such as Ober-leutnant Wilcke and Dr. Mix, Major and Oberbürgermeister of Wiesbaden, who at the beginning of the war had managed to shoot down enemy aircraft over his own town.

On 25 June 1940 the Armistice with France was signed. After the rapid capitulation of Holland and Belgium the second ''Blitz-krieg'' (lightning war) was completed. German fighter aircraft had been triumphant. Altogether 1525 aircraft had been shot down by the Luftwaffe, 854 by Flak and approximately 1900 destroyed on the ground, some in this last category by the Bf 109. During that period approximately 200 Bf 109s were lost. The most successful fighter wings in this campaign were I./JG 2 with 123 kills, III./JG 53 with 99 kills and I./JG 1 with 83 kills. At the end of the campaign in the West the most successful fighter pilots, all flying Bf 109s, were:

Hauptmann Balthasar	23 kills
Hauptmann Mölders	16 kills
Hauptmann Galland	14 kills
Oberleutnant Wick	13 kills
Hauptmann Gentzen	11 kills

The loss of fighter pilots had been kept within acceptable limits. Exact figures are not available but it must be assumed that approximately 460 Bf 109 pilots were lost, some of whom, perhaps about 200, were taken captive and returned to duty after the Armistice.

How difficult the situation was for the German fighter aircraft may be judged from the fact that after the conclusion of the campaign in the West not a single new fighter group was set up. Of the 11 heavy fighter groups there were only five left as the rest had been transferred to night fighter duties. Despite this the fighters were sent

Two Bf 109 E-3s of 6./JG 26. The grey Ibex, emblem of the squadron, is clearly visible on the 71/02/65 camouflage

Bf 109 E of II./JG 27, carrying the coat of arms of its adopted city, Berlin

After a belly landing

Bf 109 E-3 with the insignia of JG 51

Bf 109 E-3 of 6./JG 52 at
Niedermendig in the Eiffel in
1940

Bf 109 E-3 of II./JG 51 in
France, 1940

Oberfeldwebel Kleß of
II./JG 54 in his Bf 109 E-3

Bf 109 E-4 of III./JG 27. In the background the Group Adjutant's aircraft

Bf 109 E of II./JG 3, shot down over France

Bf 109 Es taking off on a sortie, unit unknown

into the Battle of Britain. Meanwhile the Royal Air Force had increased its fighter strength from 57 to 67 squadrons, 12 of them night fighter squadrons.

During the campaign in France a new version of the Bf 109 had begun to be tested on the front line. A Bf 109 E had been converted as a fighter reconnaisance aircraft. The cannon armament had been taken out completely and only two MG 17s were left. An automatic reconnaissance camera was installed in the fuselage instead. The reason for this development was the fact that the Henschel Hs 126 which had been used for short range reconnaissance no longer met requirements. Tests were carried out by 2 Staffel or Aufklärungsgruppe 21, an army reconnaissance squadron. Walter Krauß, at that time Oberleutnant, was so successful in these front line

Another Bf 109 E 4./JG 77 with make-do camouflage

tests that on 29 July 1940 he was the first reconnaissance pilot to receive the Ritterkreuz. The first fighter reconnaissance version of the Bf 109 to be series built was the Bf 109 E-5.

The Bf 109 E-5 was the first series-built fighter reconnaissance aircraft in the Luftwaffe

3. Battle of Britain (Bf 109 E-4)

Further improvements were necessary on the Bf 109 E-3 airframe, particularly with regard to armament following service experience gained during the French campaign. The disadvantage of the integral MG/FF was the magazine capacity which at the time was restricted to 60 rounds. The disadvantage was even greater if it was mounted in the wings as there was space for only 45-round drums. As the MG/FFM (the motor cannon) produced serious vibration, it was dropped and the installation of the MG/FF in the wings was improved. In other respects the airframe of the Bf 109 E-3 remained basically unchanged. There was a smooth transition from the E-3 series in the Autumn of 1940 to the E-4 series, without a test aircraft being built. The E-4 was built in the Messerschmitt factory and also under licence elsewhere.

At the same time Fieseler started the construction of a pre-series of ten carrier-based Bf 109 T-0 fighters, as it had been decided in July 1940 that the "Graf Zeppelin" aircraft carrier (19250 tons, launched 8 December 1938) should be completed. Trägergruppe 186 was intended for carrier service and was later renamed Jagdgruppe 186. When the construction of the aircraft carrier was finally cancelled, the Bf 109 Ts which had already been produced were transferred to I./JG 77 which had been

formed from J. Gr. 186 of which Major Seegert was Kommandeur in 1940. The Bf 109 T-0 had an increased wingspan, up from 9.87m to 11.06m. The wings could be folded manually for packing the aircraft in carrier hangars. The fuselage had been locally reinforced to take additional loads from by catapult fittings and arrestor hooks. In other respects this version was the same as the Bf 109 E-3. A small airfield in Drontheimfjord of the same size as an aircraft carrier deck was prepared for service testing by I./JG 77. This solution had been chosen as the military airfields in Norway generally only had very short runways. The pilots had just got used to the special features of the Bf 109 T-0 and were very satisfied with its qualities when they had to surrender the aircraft to an Erprobungskommando proving group and return to their usual Bf 109 E-3s. Major Seegert informed the author that the Bf 109 T-1 used by his group (60 were produced in all) had the increased wing span but no aircraft carrier fittings.

These Bf 109 T-1s were allocated to JG 5 but at a later date they were all converted to Bf 109 T-2s as the construction of the aircraft carrier had been cancelled and they did not go into service until 1942. Apart from their increased span they were identical to the Bf 109 E-4 B and were powered by the

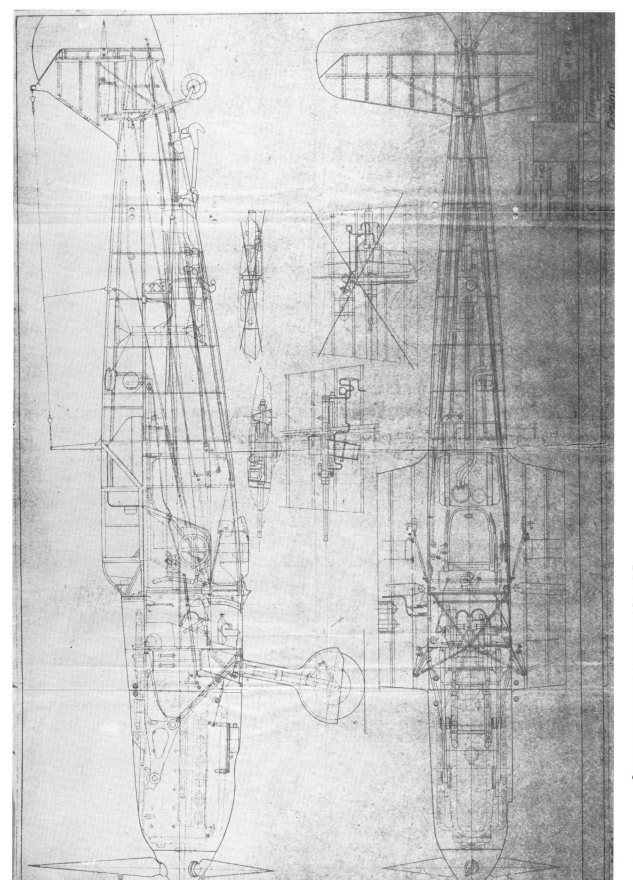

Cutaway drawing of fuselage of Bf 109 T

DB 601N of 1175PS. The ETC 250 stores carrier could either take an SC 250 bomb or a 300 litre capacity drop tank. In all, 70 Bf 109 Ts were built. The 109 E-4 B was produced as a fighter bomber version, also used in 1940 during the Battle of Britain, and its payload was that of the Bf 109 E-1B, but in other respects it was the same as the E-4.

There is no shortage of authoritative literature on the extent and the significance of the Battle of Britain and the background to it. It is just worth noting here that the dates arbitrarily allocated to it by the British do not match the facts as the increased air of-fensive by the Luftwaffe started before 10 July 1940. Apart from the reduction caused by weather conditions in Autumn and Winter of 1940/41, the Luftwaffe continued the offensive through to the withdrawal of Luftwaffe forces for Operation "Barba-rossa" in 1941, so it did continue after 31 October 1940.

This increased air offensive against Britain required Air Fleets 5 (Norway), 2 (Northeast France, Belgium and Holland) and 3 (the rest of France) and they had the following Me 109 formations at their disposal:

Luftflotte 5 Norway, Generaloberst Stumpf:

II./JG 77	Major Hentschel	Stavanger, Drontheim

Luftflotte 2 Brussels, Generalfeldmarschall Kesselring:

II./LG 2	Major Weiß	Monchy-Breton/St. Omer
Jaffü 2	General Major Osterkamp	Wissant
Stab and I.-III./JG 3	Oberst Viek from 21.8 Major Lützow	Airfields: Samer, Grandvilliers, Desvres
Stab and I.-III./JG 26	Oberstleutnant Handrick later Major Galland	Airfields: Audembert, Marquise, Caffiers
Stab and I.-III./JG 51 + IV. = I./JG 77	Major Mölders	Wissant (later Pihen) Airfields: Pihen, Marquise, St. Omer
Stab and I.-III./JG 52 + I./LG 2	Major von Merhart	Coquelles Airfields: Coquelles, Peuplingue, Calais-Marck
Stab and I.-III./JG 54	Major Mettig, later Major Trautloft	Campagne/Guines Airfields: Guines, Hermelinghen

Luftflotte 3 Paris, Generalfeldmarschall Sperrle:

Jafü 3	Oberst Junck	Deauville
Stab and I-III./JG 2	Oberstleutnant von Bülow later Major Schellmann	Evreux-Beaumont-le-Roger Airfields: Beaumont-le-Roger, Le Havre

Stab and I.-III./JG 53	Oberstleutnant von Cramon later Major von Maltzahn	Cherbourg, later Etaples Airfields: Rennes, Le Touquet, Dinan, Guernsey, Sempy, Brest
Stab and I.III./JG 27	Oberst Ibel	Cherbourg-West Airfields: Plumetot/Caen, Guines, Crépon, Fiennes Carquebut

and in Germany there remained:

Stab and III./JG 77	Major von Manteuffel	Döberitz
III./JG 52	Major von Winterfeld	Zerbst
Stab JG 1	Obesrt Schumacher	Jever

Twenty-five fighter groups flying Bf 109s were on alert for direct attack against England. Theoretically they had approximately 1200 Bf 109 Es, in fact they probably had approximately 200 machines less than that actually serviceable. On the other side the Fighter Command of RAF had approximately 600 Hurricanes and Spitfires at this time and also 100 other first line fighters. In addition there were 230 other single-seater fighters in reserve for immediate use and 700 which were undergoing repair or in the fighter pilot training schools. So it would appear that the German side had slightly more aircraft. However if you take into account the production figures of both countries in the decisive months of 1940 and in the whole of 1940 things do look rather different.

During 1940 a total of 1693 Bf 109s were manufactured. In Britain 4283 fighter aircraft, mainly Hurricanes and Spitfires were produced and in addition to them there were 219 fighters from Canada, Hurricanes and a few American types which could only be used for fighter pilot training. In the critical months in 1940 the aircraft manufactured were as follows:

in Germany (only Bf 109)	
June	164
July	220
August	173
September	218
October	200
in total	975 Bf 109 E

in England (all fighter aircraft)	
June	446
July	496
August	476
September	467
October	469
in total	2354 fighter aircraft (of which approximately 2100 were Hurricanes and Spitfires)

This shows quite clearly that the British were definitely in a position to make good their fighter aircraft losses whereas in Germany even at this early stage of the war there were bottlenecks in the production of single seat fighter aircraft. The production of Bf 110 heavy fighters (1083 in 1940) was not enough to compensate for this as it became apparent in the weeks to follow that the

Bf 109 B-2
experimentally
catapult-launched

Bf 109 E-3 of 1./JG 3
flying over the
English Channel

This Bf 109 E-3 of
2./JG 2 almost made
it to the French coast

Bf 109 E-4 of II./JG 3 during the Battle of Britain

Major Adolf Galland, the new Kommodore of JG 26 in his Bf 109 E during the Battle of Britain. Note the gun sight through the windscreen

Above: From September, 1940 the lion's head was the emblem of 6./JG 26. Below: This photograph of a Bf 109 E with 28 kills to its credit was taken at an airfield in the Protectorate of Bohemia & Moravia in 1940

Above: Bf 109 E-4 of III./JG 27 ready for a mission. Below: Bf 109 E-4 of JG 26 taxiing out

Lieutnant J. Fözö
II./JG 51 (†3.3.1979)
had Mickey Mouse as
his personal insignia

Bf 109 E-4 of II./JG 51
standing by in
Desvrès, 1940

The "White 2" of
Feldwebel Illner,
II./JG 51 during the
Battle of Britain

Two Bf 109 E-4s of
II./JG 51 over the
Channel (Feldwebel
Illner in the lead
aircraft)

In his role as
Commander of III./JG
26 Major Galland flew
this Bf 109 E-4

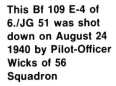

This Bf 109 E-4 of
6./JG 51 was shot
down on August 24
1940 by Pilot-Officer
Wicks of 56
Squadron

Opposite, top to bottom: Bf 109 E-3 works no. 1304 from II./JG 54. Royal Air Force No. AE 479, Bf 109 E-3B, works No. 4101. RAF No. DG 200 ex I./JG 51 being test flown during the war and renovated after the war at St. Athan, Wales

Above and below: Bf 109 E-4 of Major Wick, Kommodore JG 2, during the Battle of Britain

Opposite: Battle of Britain, 1940: Top: Bf 109 E-4 of I./JG 54. Bottom: Bf 109 E-4 shot down over France (JG 53)

Top, right: Bf 109 E-4 of I./JG 77. Top left and above: Bf 109 E-4 of JG 77 in Varnes

Bf 110 was not really a long range fighter at all. After a few days there was clear proof that the Bf 110 itself needed a fighter escort. As early as the summer of 1940 it was clear that the Bf 110 could only be used in the West European theatre as a ground attack aircraft and as a night fighter. It was still perfectly usable in the Mediterranean and later also in Russia.

But the English had another advantage. They had a very effective radio direction system (RADAR) which was continually being improved and extended and which was able to locate German air attack at a very early stage. Secondly of course they were fighting over home ground. This phase of the war demonstrated with devasting clarity that the decision to concentrate on one type of fighter, the limited range of Bf 109, which at this time could only be used for defence of Germany, had been wrong. Galland, later Inspekteur der Jagdflieger, at that stage still Group Kommandeur and later Kommodore of JG 26, stated very clearly in his book "Die Ersten und die Letzten" the problems which the original design faults in the Bf 109 had caused: "Problem number one was the inadequate range of the Bf 109 and therefore also of the formations which it was to escort. Assuming 30 minutes duration to reach the English coast and the same to return, German fighter pilots were left with just about 20 minutes time to engage the enemy. Consequently their dogfights were always limited by the pressure of time. It meant that air attack always had to use the shortest route with no attempt at diversionary tactics and this meant that their routes were always the same. Consequently the enemy knew exactly where the Bf 109 formations would be coming from. Usually the aircraft returned to base on the last dregs of the fuel so that if they were

victorious there was not even enough fuel for a victory roll. Ditching in the English Channel inevitably meant that the aircraft was lost and usually the pilot too. This accounted for a large proportion of the German losses. Damage to the engine or the airframe also generally meant the loss of man and machine. The German forces could only advance to the limit of the Bf 109. That meant that the production of fighter aircraft in Britain could continue at full speed beyond the range of the Bf 109". There is no doubt that some of the pilots who ditched in the Channel were rescued by the well-organised Luftwaffe rescue service but in every case the aircraft was lost. Galland describes very clearly just how catastrophic the minimal range of the 109 was; "Without any intervention on the part of the enemy, 12 aircraft from the squadron were lost on one sortie. Five of them managed to reach French beaches on the last drop of fuel and seven others had to ditch in the Channel."

The second problem for German fighter pilots was escort protection for bombers and dive bomber formations, which caused serious controversy time and time again. The bomber pilots demanded direct fighter escort and that meant the Bf 109 had to wait until the opponent attacked. Consequently the enemy always sought out the most favourable point of attack. After a lot of controversy a compromise solution was finally reached but it satisfied nobody.

At the end of August a lot of dead wood was cut out of the German fighter groups and many of the older commanders were bitter about it. But Luftwaffe command wanted younger Kommodores and Gruppenkommandeurs who would not be as cautious as the older men but would attack ruthlessly. The concentrated attack by the German Luftwaffe on the English fighters

CA + NK was the first
fighter bomber Bf 109
E-1B

A SC 100 bomb under
the fuselage of a Bf
109 E-1B

109

A pilot and squadron emblem of 3. LG 2 during the attacks on England.

III. Schlacht (ground attack) of LG 2 (Lehrgeschwader = training group) flew continuous fighter bomber missions from Calais-Marcke to England in the Autumn of 1940

The "Weiβe 2" (White 2) flown by Feldwebel Illner of II./JG 51, seen here over the English Channel. Illner was the son of pioneer aviator Karl Illner who test flew the Etrich-Taube.

and their bases led to a serious crisis in British Fighter Command. The loss of pilots could no longer be made up. In addition, aircraft losses increased to such an extent that even old Gloster Gladiator biplanes had to be sent into battle. Britain found that help came from a quarter it could never have expected – namely from Hitler himself. The critical error in German leadership was basically caused by German bombers making a navigational error, inadvertently ending up over the City of London and unfortunately hitting a church. Up to that point there had been a sort of gentleman's agreement: the Germans didn't attack London, the British didn't attack Berlin. But now, on the assumption that the Germans had broken the gentleman's agreement, there were three RAF air raids on Berlin one after the other. Hitler's reaction was predictable: he ordered concentrated air raids on London exactly at the moment when the British air defences were on the point of collapse. From now on the German fighters were backing a loser. In addition there was a new problem: The Stuka dive-bombers had to be withdrawn from the Front because of high losses.

The bombers were suffering high losses during daylight raids and could now only be used for night raids, so the decision was taken to send fighters across the Channel as fighter bombers. German fighter wings converted Staffel 2, 5 and 8 or 2, 6 and 7 to the Bf 109 E-4B. At the beginning of October there were already about 250 Bf 109 E-4Bs in operation. The British were taken by surprise by the fighter bomber raids. But they very soon learnt to cope with them.

German fighter pilots were by no means happy with this role. They were also untrained for the task as proper fighter bomber training didn't exist at that time. Many young fighter bomber pilots who had never before dropped a live bomb found themselves heading towards England on their first raid. There was no question of accuracy on these first raids. The pilot would approach the target and then release the bomb hopefully. The British maintain that the Battle of Britain ended in drizzle. But the battle was not finished. No-one would question that the Battle of Britain had ended to the disadvantage of the German Luftwaffe. But discussion about the RAF losses still continues as the British have not yet opened up their original records and documentation to scrutiny and so far nobody, not even a neutral observer, has had access to them. The losses suffered by the German Bf 109 formations can be calculated fairly accurately on the basis of a secret survey by the General Quartermaster of the Luftwaffe. Before July and August 1940 502 fighters were lost through enemy engagement and 98 without encountering the enemy, in all 600. If you take into account the output of 811 new Bf 109s during the same period the conclusion is inevitable that the fighter wings could not be reinforced because in addition to the write-offs it is necessary to add at least another 300 aircraft which could not be repaired in the field because of serious damage and had to be returned to the repair shops. So by the end of 1940 there wasn't a single German fighter group with a complete complement of 100 aircraft.

4. From the Bf 109 E to the Bf 109 F
The 109 gets a Fresh Image

The air offensive continued through November 1940 although daylight raids were at a reduced level. But there were already clear indications that the war was going to be extended into new areas. In the Mediterranean there were repeated clashes between the Italian and the British fleets – in which the Italians always came off worse. At the end of July 1940 Hitler made known to the Commander in Chief of the army, Generalfeldmarschall von Brauchitsch, and his Chief of Staff, Generaloberst Halder, his resolve to invade Russia in the Spring of 1941. Russia had annexed the Baltic States, which on the basis of the Non-Aggression Pact of 1939 were supposed to be German spheres of influence, and was also making further claims in the Mediterranean area.

In the middle of September the Italians attacked the British in North Africa. On 23 October the Italians attacked Greece via Albania. After severe defeats both these operations rapidly became catastrophes for the Italians. Hitler decided to respond to Mussolini's calls for aid. At the end of the year the German leaders were already beginning to have a presentiment of what lay ahead. Meanwhile at Messerschmitt work was going ahead on continued development of the Bf 109. Experience to date had shown that the performance of the aircraft in range, climb and speed needed to

be improved because there was no new German fighter aircraft in the offing. It was true that Kurt Tank, the Technical Chief of Focke-Wulf in Bremen, had produced a new design for a fighter as early as 1938 but that the RLM had not shown any great interest in it. The decision had been made to rely on the Bf 109. When in 1939 it then became clear that production of the Bf 109 was not adequate the RLM suddenly put pressure on Focke-Wulf to speed up development of the new fighter, the Fw 190. It was realised just how serious a mistake had been made.

The FW 190 V1 had flown as early as 1 June 1939. Then the difficulties started. Most of these were associated specifically with the engine. The first engine, the BMW 139, proved to be unusable. There was then a new development from BMW, the BMW 801, but the BMW 801 had problems too. Time and time again the aircraft returned from test flights belching smoke and stinking through overheating. It was only through the efforts of Focke-Wulf, the test pilots at Rechlin and two officers of Jagdgeschwader 26 that the Fw 190 finally became operational in August 1941.

Given these problems there was a need to modify the Bf 109 constantly and to improve it to the limits. But one weakness the Bf 109 could not escape: restricted fuel capacity severely limited its range of operation.

It was due to be used operationally in Africa but for this it had to be tropicalised and the fighter bomber had to be improved. And so by the end of 1940 the following new versions had been produced:

Bf 109 E-4N: Similar to E-4 but with 1175 PS DB 601N. A number of these aircraft were fitted with dust filters and emergency equipment for desert operations and were first allocated to the I./JG 27 in North Africa.

E-5: Similar to the E-3 but with no cannon, only two MG 17s. Rb 50/30 series topographic camera fitted in the fuselage behind the cockpit.

E-6: Airframe and equipment as the E-4N, armament and Rb camera as E-5.

E-7: Fighter similar to the E-4N but rack for 300 litre drop tank under fuselage. Extended range, reduced speed.

E-7/U2: Fighter bomber for use in Africa. ETC 250 release for one SC 250 or ER 4 with four SC 50s. Reinforced armour plating for cockpit engine and radiator.

E-7Z: As E-7 but with GM 1 system (methanol injection for short term performance boost).

E-8: Last higher version but in the E series. Based on flying experience gained in the Battle of Britain it was given a more powerful engine (DB 601E 1350 PS) and reinforced armour plating behind cockpit seat.

E-9: Fighter reconnaissance aircraft similar to E-8, but only two MF 17s and fitted with Rb 50/30 camera.

Encounters with the British Hurricane and Spitfire had shown that although the 109 was faster, the other types were more manoeuvrable because of their lower wing loading. The Hurricane had been designed at the same time as the 109 but was clearly inferior to it. The opposite was true of the Spitfire. Its

designer, Mitchell, had shown what performance can be achieved from an aircraft with careful aerodynamic airframe design. Messerschmitt had had to compromise between aerodynamic considerations on the one hand, RLM armament requirements and rationalised production methods on the other. He had certainly gone to great lengths to produce an aerodynamically successful airframe but this was not his prime consideration. The Bf 109 E airframe imposed certain limitations with regard to the installation of more powerful power plants and these limits had now been reached. If the intention was to produce increased performance then it was time to design a new airframe with aerodynamic efficiency as the main criterion. With hindsight it is amazing that the limited radius of action was not extended. Oberst Pasewaldt, Chief of the Development Section in the Technical Office of the RLM, explained to the author how he had suggested to Messerschmitt the need for a new fighter with increased range but that Messerschmitt had insisted on his concept of a small lightweight fighter and according to Pasewaldt he had said: "I can build you a fighter or I can build you a barn door!" Fuel tank capacity was increased by 100 litres to 400 litres but the 150 PS more powerful DB 601E had a higher fuel consumption than its predecessor, with the result that the range was not increased to any noticeable extent. If a more powerful engine was installed (the DB 605 was already under development) then the extra litres of fuel in the tank were very quickly accounted for by higher fuel consumption.

Two test aircraft were built for the new series: Bf 109 V23, works number 5603 and V24, works number 5604, VK + AB. The V24 was built first and incorporated changes to the fuselage, engine and tail but the wing

Left: Bf 109 E-7/U2 of
III/JG 1 with SC 100
Below: Bf 109 E-4B of
10./JG 26 returning
from a fighter bomber
mission over England

was unchanged, from that of the E series. In the meantime however a new wing had been developed. Wind tunnel tests had shown that using this wing the performance of the new aircraft could be enhanced. The V23 received this wing. The maiden flight of V24 took place on 10 July 1940 with that of V23 a few days afterwards. The Bf 109 F series which resulted from these two test aircraft differed from the E version mainly in the following respects: the DB 601 was completely re-cowled; the airscrew was of reduced diameter and had a large spinner which was more aerodynamically faired in with the cowling. The wing radiators used for boundary layer suction. The tailplane which had previously been strutted was now a cantilever design. The new wings had round tips and somewhat wider span than the E version. The slotted ailerons were replaced with Frise-ailerons and normal flaps of smaller area to replace the previous slotted flaps.

Test results were pleasing as there was a considerable improvement in performance.

The 109 F-0 pre-series went into immediate production. The changes had however resulted in one disadvantage: the Bf 109 F now had only one motor cannon and no wing-mounted cannons. This meant a considerable reduction in fire power. The design changes had succeeded in increasing the air speed of the E series by 25-28mph but did this justify the loss in fire power? Judging by further developments this question must have been answered in the negative because it soon became apparent that there was no option but to increase the armament of the new Bf 109 at the expense of spoiling the clean aerodynamic lines of the airframe.

When the first Bf 109 F-1s went into active service in January 1941 the result was catastrophic: within a few weeks four aircraft crashed whilst flying at maximum speed. Investigation of the pieces of wreckage showed that in all four cases parts of the tailplane were missing.

As already mentioned in 'Background to the 109', similar problems had arisen with the M29 and the M20. Resonance tests were now set up and to everyone's surprise it was discovered that on reaching a certain speed range the ever-present vibration increased to such an extent that the tailplane broke up. Up to series E the tailplane had been strutted. In the F series the tailplane struts had been deleted from the design without adequate strengthening of the tailplane structure. The tailplane was now further reinforced and the Bf 109 F-1 began to go into active service. The aircraft met with a mixed reception. On the one hand the wing-mounted cannons had often been unreliable and had also produced vibration in certain conditions in flight, but on the other hand the Me 109 E-4's armament of three cannons was missed. Werner Mölders, at that time Kommodore of JG 51, accepted the Bf 109 F from the very beginning but Adolf Galland, Kommodore of JG 26 and Oesau of JG 2 kept their E-4s as long as they possibly could. They preferred the cannons.

As early as 1935 the Mauser firm had been working on a weapon which would replace the MG/FF. This weapon, the MG 151, was finally ready for operational use by the end of 1940. It was delivered with two different barrels, 15mm calibre or, as the MG 151/20, 20mm. As a motor cannon the MG 151/20 developed a muzzle velocity of 790m/sec and had a fire rate of 550-750 rounds per minute. This weapon was to become one of the most widely used aircraft mounted weapons. In normal non-

Pre-production prototypes for the F series: Above Bf 109 V23 Below: Bf 109 V24, works no. 5604

synchronised form its performance was even higher.

One of the first pre-series Bf 109 F-0s had been flown operationally by Oberstleutnant Werner Mölders (at that time still Kommodore of JG 51) in October 1940. His report was clear: the speed of the Bf 109 F-0 was approximately the same as the Spitfire II which was used over the Channel at that time. In turns the Spitfire II was better. But in a straight climb the Bf 109 F was better. The Spitfire could turn more sharply. Excessive "G" forces in tight turns or when coming out of the dive were inadvisable in the 109: the Bf 109 F would sometimes "clap hands" – the wings would break off or at least develop creases parallel to the direction of flight. One of the most successful fighter pilots of that time, Hauptmann Balthasar, was killed under exactly these circumstances. On 3 July 1941 he lost his life when his aircraft crashed after the wings broke off.

Mölders was of the opinion that the range was still inadequate. At the beginning of February 1941 the battle over the Channel resumed at a more intense level. On 22 February, Bf 109 E-4B and E-7 fighter bombers began making sorties across the Channel. The fighter bombers were generally in the 10.Wing of the fighter groups. These fighter bomber raids generally had fighter escort so there were often dogfights between Bf 109s and Spitfires. The Spitfires soon recognized fighter bombers and tried to single them out in the German formations.

German fighter pilots had a nasty surprise in March 1941. The Royal Air Force had had the opportunity to fly two Bf 109 Es which had been captured in France, and on the basis of their findings had drawn the necessary conclusions and developed a new Spitfire – the new Mk. V. The Spitfire Mk. III never went into series production –

only two were built – and the Spitfire Mk. IV was only a fighter reconnaissance aircraft. The British had worked fast, as they had to, to overcome the superiority of the Bf 109. 23 Mk. I and Mk. II Spitfires were modified for installation of the new Rolls-Royce "Merlin 45". These aircraft were then sent immediately to the Channel.

The first Mk. V Spitfires still had the old armament of eight machine guns, which meant they were not as well armed as the Bf 109. They were more manoeuvrable and could climb faster than the Bf 109 E which was still in operational use. The armament problem was solved with the Spitfire Mk. VB which was soon operational with two 20mm calibre Hispano-Suiza cannons and four 7.62mm machine guns. It was therefore considerably better armed than the Bf 109 E and even the new Bf 109 F. The Spitfire FB Mk. V (fighter bomber) had clipped wings, which made it faster but reduced its performance in climb. But the pure fighter version was superior to the Bf 109 F in every respect.

During the first week of June 1941 certain fighter wings were withdrawn from the Channel coast and transferred to the East for Operation "Barbarossa", the invasion of Russia. In the West only the following Bf 109 formations remained:

Stab and I. to III. Gruppe JG 2 "Richthofen"
Stab and I. to III. Gruppe JG 26 "Schlageter"
I. Group JG 51

and in addition the replacement groups of JG 2, 3, 26 and 53 with one to two squadrons. That means there were 300 Bf 109s at most confronting the strong formations of RAF Fighter Command and Bomber Command.

It is also worth noting that JG 26 was short

of the 7th squadron under Oberleutnant Jochen Müncheberg. This squadron had been transferred to Gela, Sicily on 9 February as part of the German aid to Italy in North Africa. The X. Fliegerkorps under General der Flieger Geisler had the task of taking the island fortress of Malta and defeating the British fleet in the Mediterranean. Up to that point it had only the III./ZG 26 under Hauptmann Kaschka with three squadrons of Bf 110 D and the 1st squadron of Nachtjagdgeschwader 3 (night fighter group) under Oberleutnant Peters with Ju 88 C-2s and Ju 88 C-4s. Müncheberg and his dozen Bf 109 E-7s carried out a cull of the Hurricanes based on Malta. Between 12th and 28th February a dozen Hurricanes were shot down without loss of Bf 109s. In January the British had only 12 Hurricanes. Now they made great efforts to bring up reinforcements.

Italian defeats during the ill-considered invasion of Greece and the coup d'état in Yuyoslavia forced Hitler to postpone his offensive against Russia. First he had to sort out the Balkan problems.

In the meantime development proceeded on the Bf 109 F. To give at least a temporary advantage over the new Spitfire several Bf 109 F-2s were fitted with GM-1 systems and designated Bf 109 F-2Z. It would appear that some Bf 109 F-2Zs were converted to fighter bombers using R3 field modification kits, as on 11 May 1941 the British reported a fighter bomber attack by "bomb-carrying Me 109 Fs" on the English fighter bases at Lympne and Hawkinge. During these raids one of the Bf 109 Fs was shot down by a Spitfire V of 91st squadron. The series-produced Bf 109 F-4B only came into service in 1942. British reports at that time stressed that the Bf 109 F was generally able to climb so high that it could then attack the Spitfire from superior altitude. By that time the Hurricanes were pathetically vulnerable to the Bf 109.

Bf 109 F-0, PH + BE

Müncheberg's 7./JG 26 on Sicily, 1941. Above: A Bf 109 E-7; on the right an Italian Fiat CR 42. Below: Bf 109 E-7 with 300 litre drop tank

Above: Jochen Müncheberg with his yellow 12. Below: another pilot in the squadron. The squadron emblem, ace of hearts and the group emblem "S" easily recognisable

Pilot of 7./JG 26 enthusing over his last dog fight.

In the meantime the storm in the Balkans had gathered. For the Balkan campaign the following Bf 109 formations were made available, generally flying Bf 109 F-2s:

Stab JG 54	Major Trautloft	Operational base: Graz
II./JG 54	Hptm. Hrabak	Operational base: Graz
III./JG 54	Hptm. Lignitz	Operational base: Arad
I/JG 27	Hptm. Neumann	Operational base: Graz
Stab JG 27	Major Schellmann	Operational base: Belica/Bulgaria
II./JG 27	Hptm. Lippert	Operational base: Vrba
III./JG 27	Hptm. Dobislav	Operational base: Belica
Stab JG 77	Major Woldenga	Operational base: Deta/Temesvar
II./JG 77	Hptm. Lange	Operational base: Deta/Temesvar
III./JG 77	Major v. Winterfeld	Operational base: Deta/Temesvar
I./LG 2	Hptm. Ihlefeld	Operational base: Deta/Temesvar

Kept in reserve and to protect the Rumanian oil fields was

III./JG 52	Major Handrick	Operational base: Bucharest-Pipera

The invasion of Yugoslavia followed the lines of previous Blitzkriegs and was soon over. For a short while the Dornier Do 17 Ka-2 bombers and Messerschmitt Bf 109 E-3s which had earlier been sold to Yugoslavia produced some nasty surprises.

Dogfights were common between Yugoslavian Bf 109 E-3s and the German Bf 109 F-2. But the Yugoslavians' lack of combat experience made them relatively easy prey for the German fighter pilots. They presented an unpleasant threat to army units however which naturally could not tell at first glance whether the low-flying Bf 109 was Yugoslavian or German, and in some cases this led to heavy losses.

The war in Greece was difficult because of the small and cramped grass airfields. Overcrowding frequently caused significant losses of fighter aircraft on take-off and landing.

Fighting in Greece was over by the end of April 1941. The British admitted to losing 64 aircraft to the German Bf 109 in Greece during the period 6 to 30 April. The Bf 109s also destroyed a further 87 British aircraft on the ground.

Then preparations began for the landing on Crete. JG 77 under Major Woldenga remained behind on Molai on the southern tip of the Peloponnese as the only fighter formation for this operation. On 14 May JG 77 together with the Bf 110s of ZG 26 carried out a low level attack on the British airfields on Crete and two Bf 109s were shot down by flak. There was little air combat over Crete as the British only had a few Hurricanes stationed there. The main operations were carried out by fighter bombers of III./JG 77 and I./LG 2. Oberleutnant Huy with a group of III./JG 77 succeeded in putting all the starboard gun turrets of the

123

British battleship "Warspite" (31,100 t) out of action with two direct hits. This earned Huy the Ritterkreuz. Here too it was Bf 109 Fs with ETC 250 bomb releases which were successful. Unfortunately the pilots of two other fighter bombers belonging to I./LG 2 were reported missing presumed dead. One of these discovered the British cruiser "Fiji" (8000 t) south of Crete but his fuel was already very low. In spite of heavy flak he attacked the vessel and holed the side of the ship with a 260kg bomb. Half an hour later a second Bf 109 appeared and scored a direct hit on the cruiser's boiler room, again with an SC 250. The boiler exploded, the cruiser capsized and sank. It was not often that Bf 109 fighers bombers were as successful as that.

The fighter pilots in the Balkan expedition were remarkably successful. For a loss of only 20 Bf 109s, 167 English, Greek and Yugoslavian aircraft were shot down.

In the middle of April the three squadrons of I./JG 27 under Major "Edu" Neumann arrived on the desert airstrip Ain-el-Gazalla.

This group was equipped with the Bf 109 E-4N *trop.* which was generally superior to the British Hurricane IIs. This group then became the Afrika Gruppe under young Leutnant Hans-Joachim Marseille from Berlin, just as the whole of JG 27, when it was transferred to Africa, became the "Afrika Geschwader". It was a strange coincidence that Neumann's group had already sported on their aircraft a symbol that seemed almost like a premonition of their fate: a circle containing the approximate outline of Africa, a negro head and a lion. This symbol was inherited from Neumann's predecessor Hauptmann Riegel, who was an enthusiastic supporter of German colonialism. The first squadron of JG 27 had similar success. On 19 April they shot down four Hurricanes. On 25 April Fähnrich Marseille had his first kill in Africa, a Hurricane, followed by a Blenheim on 28 April. By 2 May the British had recorded the loss of 22 Hurricanes in combat. This was against the loss of four Bf 109s. The British then reinforced their fighter formations to five Hurricane squadrons and an additional one equipped with Curtiss H.75s delivered from the United States. The battle in the air was intensified on 15 June with the British offensive to relieve the beleaguered Tobruk. When General Wavell had to discontinue fighting the British had already lost one-third of their fighters, 33 of them, in combat. In addition to I./JG 27, Oberleutnant Müncheberg and six Bf 109s from 7./JG 26 based in Sicily flew over as reinforcements and were responsible for this success. In June the Bf 109 met fresh opposition in Africa; the Curtiss P-40 "Tomahawk" delivered to the British from the United States. The Tomahawk unsettled the Bf 109 pilots but only for a short while. They soon noticed that although the solid-looking aircraft was very manoeuvrable, it was inferior to the Bf 109 E-4N at speed, in the climb and dive.

Fighter activity was noticeably reduced in June and July. It was obvious that the British were preparing for a fresh offensive.

**Bf 109 E-7/U2 of 10.
(Jabo)/JG 27 in the
Balkan campaign**

**Fighter bomber of
III./JG 27 in Greece,
April 1941**

**Heat was a problem
during operations for
both pilots and
ground crew (Bf 109
E-7 of JG 27)**

125

Lieutnant Huy, III./JG 77; behind him a Bf 109 F-2

Hauptmann Ihlefeld, Kommodore I./LG 2, on July 12 1941, at Jassy, Rumania

Belly landing by Adjutant of III./JG 77 in Rumania, 1941

Bf 109 E-9 in Augsburg before being handed over to JG 2

Bf 109 E-4s of I./JG 27 at Forli (Italy) on the way to Africa

Left: Bf 109 E-4N of I./JG 27 over Libya

Above and below: The arrival of I./JG 27 in Libya soon put a stop to British air superiority (Bf 109 E-4N)

5. 1941: Bf 109 F victorious in Russia

It was obvious even in 1940 that the Me 209 V4 was unsuitable as a fighter and work began in Augsburg on a new project, the Me 309, design work being completed in 1941. As Messerschmitt production capacity was already at its limits it was decided first of all to build a small pre-production batch of 10 aircraft. A number of fundamental changes from the Bf 109 were to be made in this design, changes for which there was no experimental evidence in support, so several Bf 109 test aircraft were converted for this purpose. Amongst the Me 309 innovations was a retractable oil and water radiator which could be extended or retracted by degrees according to cooling requirements. A mechanism had to be devised for this purpose. Also the Me 309 was to have a wide track undercarriage like the Me 209 V4, as the undercarriage difficulties with the Bf 109 had never really been satisfactorily resolved. 4 Bf 109 Fs were used for tests and flight testing of these and other innovations. They were: Bf 109 V24, works no. 5604 (VK + AB), which had already been used for the first tests on the Bf 109F, Bf 109 V30, works no. 5716 (ND + IE), V30A, works no. 5717 (ND + IF) and V31, works no. 5642 (SG + EK). The last three of these were aircraft from the F-1 series. These were fitted for the first time with a pressurized cabin with air conditioning. Needless to say a tremendous amount of time and effort had to be invested in these innovations before the construction of a pre-production batch could be started.

In addition, development on the Bf 109 itself continued and resulted in lack of time. This meant that work on the Me 309 development tended to be peripheral. The RLM seemed more interested in further development of the Bf 109 than the Me 309. No doubt the fact that the Bf 109 production figures could be increased constantly, whereas a new design would necessarily mean a reduction in production figures were critical factors. The testing of the above-mentioned pre-production prototypes for the Me 309 was completed only at the end of 1941 and then the construction of the Me 309 V1 was to begin.

In the meantime, Hitler's intensely enthusiastic preparations for the invasion of Russia were nearly completed. At the beginning of June 1941 the fighter groups intended for use on the East German front were assembled. In addition there were the fighters of Luftlotte 5 in Norway. These were 13./JG 77 under Oberleutnant Carganico which was stationed in Kirkenes, and flew Bf 109 T-2s built by Fieseler and 14./JG 77 under Oberleutnant Menzel flying Bf 109 E-7s which was still being set up.

All other fighter formations were equipped with the Bf 109 F-2. These were:

Bf 109 V23 (above) and V31 were used as test aircraft for the development of the Me 309

Me 109 V23
Fixed tricycle undercarriage,
works no. 5603

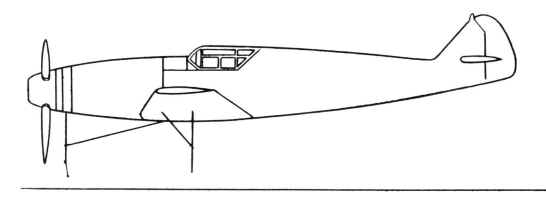

Angle to fuselage axis 0.8 degrees when spring extended
Angle to fuselage axis 1.5 degrees "taxiing"
Angle to fuselage axis 3 degrees with spring fully compressed

Drawing A14091Z
A14092Z
A14093Z
15.3.41

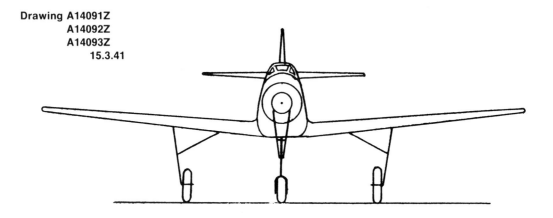

Me 109 V 23 Sketch
This aircraft that had already served as a prototype for the F-series was given a fixed tricycle undercarriage to represent the retractable undercarriage to be fitted to the Me 309. Taxiing tests showed that the nose wheel would have to be steerable for greatest manoeuvrability when taxiing. The habitual Me 109 problem of ground looping on take-off was no longer a problem. Cross wind take-offs worked well too. The nose wheel suspension proved to be too soft. In a cross wind the pressure on the main undercarriage became noticeable. In other respects taxiing qualities were good.

Luftflotte 1   North, General der Flieger Keller:

Stab and I.-III./JG 54	Major Trautloft	Operational bases in East Prussia
Erg. Gr./JG 54	Hauptmann Eggers	
II./JG 53	Hauptmann Bretnütz	

Luftflotte 2   Central, Generalfeldmarschall Kesselring

Stab and I./JG 53	Major von Maltzahn	Operational bases in Poland
IV./JG 51	Major Beckh	
Stab and I.-III/JG 51	Major Mölders	Operational bases in Poland
Stab and II. + III./JG 27	Major Schellman	Operational bases in Poland
II./JG 52	Hauptmann Woitke	
III./JG 53	Hauptmann Wilcke	

Luftflotte 4   South East, Generaloberst Löhr

Stab and III./JG 52	Major Trübenbach	Operational bases in Rumania
Stab and I.-III./JG 3	Major Lützow	Operation bases in Hungary and Poland
I./LG 2	Hauptmann Ihlefeld	
Stab and II./-III./JG 77	Obstlt. Handrick	Operation bases in Rumania
Erg.Gr./JG 77	Major Fischer	

In all, there were more than 800 Bf 109s ready for action. In addition there were also 180 Bf 110 heavy fighters. But it is worth remembering that the length of the front was nearly 3,700 miles and that there was therefore only one fighter per four miles. It was impossible, therefore, for the fighters to control airspace over the whole area of operations. It was a matter of producing a concentration of air power in a number of places. One might have assumed that new and powerful fighter formations would have been set up for the East, but there were neither the aircraft nor the pilots available. Nevertheless, the German fighter pilots were particularly successful in the new situation. What was known about the Russian Air Force and its aircraft lead one to expect that that would be the case. But one pilot, Oberst Mölders, expressed opinions at that time which gave his men food for thought when he called them together on the 20th June, 1941. Unlike the German High Command he foresaw a long and bitter battle with Russia. He predicted that many youngsters who had still not started to learn to fly would have opportunity enough to win the Ritterkreuz for success in aerial combat.

There is no doubt that the Red Air Force had obsolete equipment. The majority of the Soviet fighter formations consisted of the I-15s, I-152s and I-153s together with I-16s from Polikarpov which had already been used in Spain in 1937. The new MiG 1 and MiG 3, LaGG3 and Yak 1 were only just starting to be produced. In addition to this the Russian fighter pilots were short of combat experience. In spite of these factors it soon became apparent that even flying their old machines they knew how to make difficulties for the fast Bf 109 F2. They fought a hard and bitter battle and knew how to extract the very last ounce from their flying ability. Many a Bf 109 pilot was surprised when the I-16 he was pursuing suddenly turned on a wing tip with the result that the 109, which could only turn wider, flew straight past its victim.

Back in Germany, people were still asleep, unaware that on the morning of 23rd June 1941, at 3.15 a.m., the first grenades were dropping on to Russian territory and aircraft engines were warming up. The sheer superiority of the Bf 109 can be seen from a single daily report: III./JG 53 shot down 36 Russian aircraft on the first day of the Russian campaign and destroyed 28 on the ground. The Group Commander, Hauptmann Wilcke, shot down 5 I-15s, 3 of them in twenty minutes. The other fighter groups were equally successful. On the first day of the campaign the Luftwaffe operated almost without opposition. The death of the Commodore of JG 27, Major Schellmann was a major blow. Whilst shooting down a "Rata" (I-16) his aircraft was damaged by disintegrating parts of the enemy aircraft and he was forced to make an emergency landing. As the German troops advanced they discovered clues which proved that he had parachuted safely, been seized by Russians and probably shot. Many other German pilots who fell into Soviet hands suffered a similar fate. On the second day of the campaign there was not a single Russian fighter to be seen in the air. But then aircraft which had been freshly mobilised appeared in large numbers. Russian aircraft were shot down in their hundreds or destroyed on the ground, but the fighting was not without cost to the Germans. Many losses were caused by Bf 109 undercarriage difficulties. One group alone lost 5 Bf 109s through undercarriage collapse when landing. After one week III./JG 53 reported: "our Gruppe has only 20 serviceable aircraft left!" That meant a third of their aircraft had been lost. Regardless of losses the Russians delivered more and more aircraft to the front. It has been established that even obsolete aircraft such as the old four-engined Tupolev TB3 bomber and the Polikarpov fighter I-5 from the early thirties were used. JG 54, for example, was able to report on June 30th that for the loss of 3 of its own aircraft it had shot down 65 enemy aircraft. In the war diary entry for that day there is the somewhat surprised comment: "the enemy still has considerable numbers of bombers and fighters".

The fighter-bombers were particularly effective here too. How effective they were is seen in an entry in the war log book of JG 51: "JG 51 crushed the enemy to such an extent that the XXIV Panzerkorps were able to cross the Dnieper with hardly a single shot to deter them."

The heat had become intolerable and so too had a plague of mosquitoes. Ground staff suffered dreadfully. But the delay in the delivery of spare parts reduced the operational strength of fighter wings continually.

Even at this early stage of the Russian campaign the vulnerability of the Bf 109 on the ground was seen time and time again and was made worse by the delays in delivery of spare parts, sub-assemblies and engines. Supplies were actually the responsibility of Nachschubamt LE, which controlled supplies via the air depots. The air depot at Erding was responsible for the Bf 109.

As early as 1940/41 attempts had been made to create a supplies organisation

In the west and in the east further south, the Bf 109 F was already in active service. But in the far north, in Finland, I./JG 77 were still flying the Bf 109 E-7, Kauhara, October, 1941.

JG 54 (above) were
still flying the
Bf 109 E-4 and JG 51
were also still flying
the Bf 109 E-4. At this
stage there were
very few Bf 109 F in
active service.

Loading a bomb
under a
Bf 109 E-7

Top: Ground attack
and fighter bomber
pilots were still flying
the Bf 109 E-7 in 1941
11. (Schlacht)/LG 2

Centre and right: The
Kommodore of JG 51,
Oberst Mölders, was
already flying a
Bf 109 F-4 at the
beginning of the
Russian
campaign

Top and centre:
III./JG 52 were
amongst the first to
get the Bf 109 F-4

In August 1941 III./JG
3 also received the
Bf 109 F-4

The Bf 109 F-4 of Feldwebel Schentke, 7./JG 3

Centre: The majority of the fighter formations were concentrated in the east and just JG 2 and JG 26 remained on the English Channel. Major Galland gets ready for action. Bottom: ''Pips'' Priller, at that time Oberleutnant, was to be Galland's successor as Kommodore of JG 26 (6th from right)

It was about this time that Göring visited JG 26 in Audembert, here seen (above) with Galland and on the right Hauptmann Rothenberg. On the same occasion (below) from left to right, General Bodenschatz, Göring, Galland, Rothenberg

Hauptmann Pingel,
Kommodore of I./JG
26 was forced down
over England and
forced to land (top
and centre)

At this time
Hauptmann Rudorfer,
JG 2, already had 40
confirmed kills

within the framework of the aircraft industry, namely the *Gesellschaft für Luftfahrtbedarf* in Berlin. As there were two separate organisations, LE and the repair works which were operating more against than with each other, it didn't work. There was no major change until Udet's death on 17th November, 1941. The Reichsminister for Munitions and War Production, Albert Speer, arranged that all supplies for army, navy and airforce should be provided by autonomous bodies in the arms industry which were now set up extremely quickly. The military organisations only had to process the requirements. How these were then fulfilled was for industry itself to decide. The new system did, in fact, work very well. Intervention by the military in production, which had to some extent been arbitrary, now ceased. Only in this way was it later possible to go on increasing production. On the other hand, after the new arrangements were set up, as the author knows from his own experience, demands by repair works or air depots could be met to short deadlines from 1942 onwards. However from 1943 this became evermore difficult because of the increasing shortage of raw materials and the greater intensity of the air raids over German territory. Nevertheless, that was not the fault of the organisation which Speer had set up.

What things were like in early Autumn was shown by a report by II./JG 53 dated 18th August, 1941. On this day there were only 5 Bf 109 Fs still operational in the whole group. Just four days later 4 new Bf 109s arrived and 6 DB 601 engines. Despite everything the group achieved their 500th kill of the war on 27th August, 1941. By 30th September 1941 14,200 Soviet aircraft had been destroyed either in the air or on the ground.

The first snow fell on October 6th and took German leadership totally by surprise. Winter had really set in by the 15th October. There was 8″ of fresh snow in the north and in central areas. The German fronts in the east froze up and it is a well known fact that progress towards Moscow stopped in its tracks – only to be resumed in the spring. The success of the fighter pilots is shown from the list of the most successful German fighter pilots current at that time. Their victories were all gained flying the Bf 109:

Name	Number of Kills
Mölders†	101
Lützow	101
Oesau	100
Galland	94 (only in the west)*
Bär	88
Gollob	85
Philipp	72
Joppien†	70
Nordmann	70
von Kageneck	67
Ihlefeld	63
Hoffmann†	63
Müncheberg	62 (in the west and in the Mediterranean)
Priller	58 (only in the west)*
Wagner	57
Wick†	56 (only in the west)
Steinhoff	51
von Maltzahn	51
Beerenbrock	51

Mölders had been appointed to the post of ''General der Jagdflieger'' but then suffered a fatal crash whilst flying to be present at Udet's funeral at Breslau-Grandau.

* Some of Galland's and Priller's victories were partly achieved flying the Fw 190 as JG 26 received its first Fw 190 A-1s in August 1941.

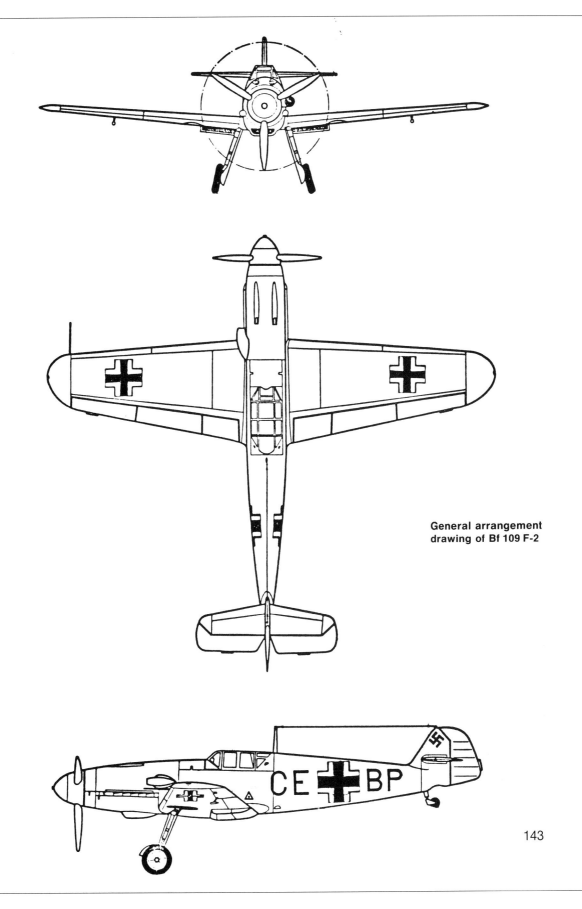

General arrangement
drawing of Bf 109 F-2

143

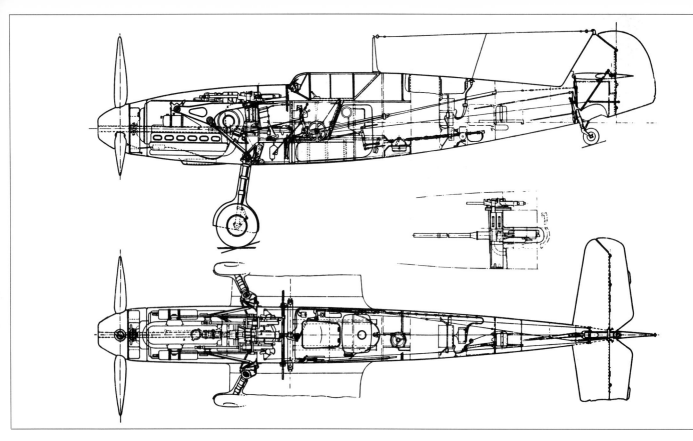

Cutaway drawing of the fuselage of the Bf 109 F-2/F-4

Bf 109 F-2s of JG 27

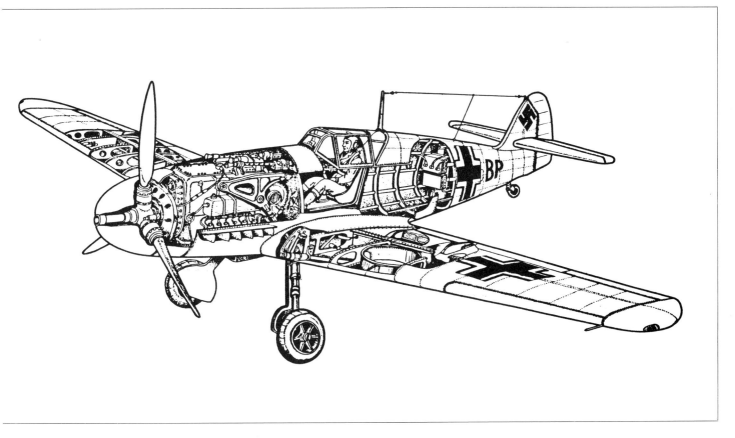

Cutaway drawing of Bf 109 F

Bf 109 F-4 of JG 54 on the eastern front

6. Africa and the Mediterranean 1941/42 Further development of the Bf 109 F

As there was still no prospect of a replacement for the Bf 109, there was no option but to continue developing the Bf 109 F. Focke-Wulf were forever modifying the Fw 190 as the BMW 801 engine was still causing problems. There was no doubt that the gap in engine development resulting from the ban on engine construction in 1919, had not been made good. In effect, the development of high performance engines had only really begun again in 1933. Admittedly, military aircraft had been built in secret from 1919 to 1932 but these were powered either by foreign engines or by the only available 600 PS engine, the BMW V/I. Then there was the question of steel. The German engines had a poor power-to-weight ratio. Anyone who has had the opportunity to compare the crankshaft of a DB 601 with that of a Rolls-Royce Merlin will know why the German engines were so heavy. The diameter of the British crankshaft was considerably less than that of the German.

In the middle of 1941 work was going ahead on installing the MG 151/20 as a motor cannon instead of the MG 151/15. In addition, it was intended to replace the 1175 PS DB 601N in the Bf 109 F-2 with the 1350 PS DB 601E. This resulted in the Bf 109 F-3 powered by the DB 601E, with MG 151/15 and 2 MG 17s, making an all-up weight of

2805kg and the Bf 109 F-4 with the same engine but the 151/20 machine gun, reinforced armour plating and fuel tank protection. In the spring of 1942 there was series production of the F-3, the F-2 and in Africa the F-2 *trop.*, and also the E-4N *trop*. Royal Air Force Bomber Command intensified night raids over Germany, but these raids were not yet as intensive as the area bombing which started a year later.

The war in North Africa was gradually turning into a war against convoys. The British controlled the supply routes to North Africa from Malta and so were able to attack the German/Italian convoys carrying supplies for Rommel. In their turn they had to keep Malta supplied and bring in reinforcements, which meant that German and Italian aircraft and the Italian navy were attacking the British convoys to Malta. The Italian navy was not particularly effective in this respect. The Regia Aeronautica was hopelessly obsolete; it fought as well as it could but was forced to be on the defensive. Tobruk was still under seige. Supplies to the garrison were difficult and cost the British Mediterranean fleet heavy losses. On the other hand the British were successful on many occasions in disrupting Axis supplies to North Africa. For example on the night of 8/9 September, 1941, 2 British cruisers and 2 destroyers sank a complete Italian convoy of

7 transport ships (39,000 tons).

On November 18th the long expected British offensive on Tobruk began – and with superior forces. In the air alone for example, 1,072 British aircraft were lined up against 120 German and 200 Italian aircraft. In the battles that followed, Marseille showed for the first time what you can do with a Bf 109. On 24 September he shot down a Maryland bomber in the morning. In the afternoon there was a confrontation over the Halfaya pass between half a dozen Bf 109s of I./JG 27, Marseille being amongst them, and about 15 to 20 Hurricanes and Tomahawks. There was a hotly contested dogfight in the course of which Marseille destroyed four enemy aircraft in fifteen minutes. His comrade Homuth shot down two enemy aircraft and a third pilot also shot one down. Three of the aircraft destroyed belonged to the 1st South African Squadron. On 27 September there was a further German success. Three fighters and two bombers were shot down in flames. At the end of September II. Gruppe of JG 27 was withdrawn from the eastern front and also transferred to North Africa. It had been equipped with brand new Bf 109 Fs in Germany. I. and II./JG 27 now jointly opposed the British and South Africans – and with some success. The reinforcements had been urgently needed as the British "Desert Air Force" had been considerably augmented: 14 fighter squadrons, 2 long-range fighter squadrons, 8 medium bomber squadrons, 3 reconnaissance squadrons and 5 heavy bomber squadrons were now lined up against the 60 or so German fighter aircraft . . .

The British stepped up activity from the middle of October 1941. Their main intention was to disable German fighter aircraft on the ground by attacking their airfield bases.

About this time I./JG 27 were sent home in batches to replace their old Bf 109 E-4Ns with the Bf 109 F-2 *trop.* This meant that at certain times there were only 4 squadrons of JG 27 actually operational. There were also difficulties affecting supplies of spare parts and fuel as the British Mediterranean Fleet was consistently preventing Italian convoys from breaking through to North Africa. As the situation in the Mediterranean gradually became more dangerous and the Eastern front was getting quieter, Hitler decided to transfer Luftlotte 2 (in fact only the 2nd Fliegerkorps) to Africa and Sicily. He did it although fighter losses alone on the eastern front since the beginning of the Russian invasion totalled 568 Bf 109s. In addition 413 Bf 109s were unserviceable because they were so severely damaged that they had to be sent back to German workshops for repair. That meant the loss of 981 Bf 109s altogether. The Luftwaffe had started with 800.

With Jagdgruppe 53 under its Kommodore Major von Maltzahn, II. Fliegerkorps under Generaloberst Bruno Loerzer also came to the Mediterranean theatre. On December 19 the group assembled in Comiso on Sicily. It was equipped with Bf 109 F-2s. The first Hurricanes were shot down over Malta on December 21. Cutting off supplies to North Africa had already enabled the British 8th Army to break through to Tobruk. On 23 December it had been necessary to yield up Benghasi. Now it was a question of capturing Malta. On 21 December II. Fliegerkorps and X. Fliegerkorps, which had already been in Sicily for some time and were therefore weakened, began concentrated attacks on Malta. It soon paid off: the Italian convoys got through without losses.

In November torrential rain had put JG 27 hors de combat for three weeks. Then the weather improved. On November 22 there were serious air battles. JG 27 Bf 109s took a group of Blenheims with Tomahawk escort by surprise one morning and shot down 4 Blenheims and 3 Tomahawks without themselves suffering any losses. But the British kept sending new formations. The battle in the air lasted all day. At nightfall the men of JG 27 could report that 13 fighters and 8 bombers had been shot down. But at some cost: 5 Bf 109s did not return. These were difficult days for I. and II./JG 27. They were worn down by lack of fuel and from exhaustion resulting from having to scramble time and time again. Then they had to retreat. Their new base was Tmimi. Here they were reinforced by III./JG 27 under Hauptmann Braune. Now the whole of JG 27 had assembled in Africa. It became the "Afrika-Geschwader".

When JG 53 transferred to Sicily, they changed the ace of spades markings on their aircraft and became known as the "Malta Group".

The situation became ever more threatening for JG 27. On 24th December 1941 the whole group only had 6 serviceable aircraft and these had to take on 40 English Curtiss fighters. In the resulting battle Oberleutnant Graf Kageneck, with 67 victories behind him, was so badly wounded that he died three weeks later.

On 7th January 1942 the British offensive was virtually over. Even the British could do no more. According to their own records they had lost 300 aircraft from the beginning of the offensive. They were totally surprised on 19 January 1942 by Rommel's fresh attack which continued until February 7 when it stopped at Ain-el-Gazala.

In the meantime JG 53 had finished off the few remaining Hurricanes over Malta. It was only now that it was decided back in Britain to deploy Spitfires abroad. The aircraft carrier "Eagle" transported the aircraft to a point from which they could just reach Malta after taking off from the flight deck. 20 March 1942 saw the first air raid on Malta. It had been planned by the Stabchef of II. Fliegerkorps, Oberst Deichmann. When the attack was continued on the following day, there were no British fighter aircraft to be seen. To reinforce the escort for the German bombers II./JG 3 had been brought in to support the 3 wings of JG 53. The raids on Malta were continued until Generalfeldmarschall Kesselring, the Commander-in-Chief South at a daily briefing at the end of April announced: "Between 20 March and 28 April 1942 Malta was completely eliminated as a naval and airforce base."

In the east the Russians had carried out a number of offensives during the winter of 1941/42 and encircling Demjansk was one of the most important results. In addition, Russian parachutists and airborne troops were beginning to become a serious danger. In spite of these factors the German front was maintained, generally speaking, although there were heavy losses. The Messerschmitts didn't have an easy time. Again and again the weakness of the Bf 109 became apparent: the undercarriage was too narrow and often led to crashes on landing, and the tendency of the Bf 109 to groundloop when taking off or landing added to the difficulties of the frozen ground and the limited range of the aircraft.

On the other hand on February 12 1942 German fighter aircraft were very successful in the west in "Operation Cerberus" (codeword for fighter escort accompanying the breakthrough of the battleships "Scharnhorst" and "Gneisenau" and the heavy cruiser "Prinz Eugen" up the English Channel). Skilful leadership meant that the

I./JG 27 under Major "Edu" Newmann were still flying the Bf 109 E

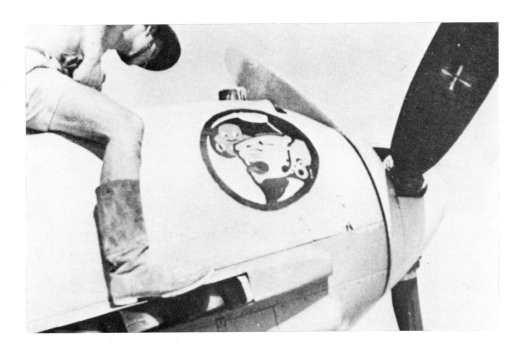

At this time Oberleutnant Stahlschmidt (left) had 48 kills credited on his fin. And so did Leutnant Marseille

JG 53, stationed on Sicily, would while away the time between sorties playing Skat . . . the cockpit of the Bf 109 F-4 being protected from the heat. Primitive but effective!

Bf 109 F-4 of JG 53 takes off on a sortie. The white circle around the rear fuselage was carried by aircraft operating in the Mediterranean. Below: A Bf 109 F-4 B of the Regia Aeronautica (Italy)

JG 53 were deployed in North Africa for a time as well (Bf 109 F4 *trop.*)

Bf 109 F-2 *trop.* of I./JG 27 with 300 litre drop tank

A shot-down Bf 109 F-2 *trop.* of 7./JG 27 (III Gruppe)

Aircraft of III./JG 27 abandoned through lack of fuel

The old Bf 109 E-7 was
still being flown in the
far north in May, 1942,
seen here in Alakurtti,
Finland

Bf 109 E-7 with
7./JG 5 in Banak
between Bodö and
Petsamo

New pilots were trained both in Germany and in occupied territories: Leutnant Wenk, Schlachtfliegerschule (ground attack fighter school), Reims (Bf 109 F)

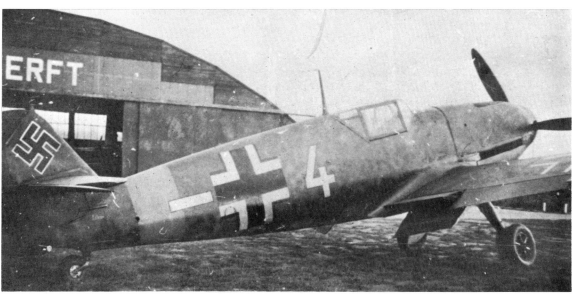

Bf 109 F-4 Fliegerschule 126 (Pilot Training School) Stübbendorf b/Oppeln

Pair of Bf 109 F-2s from Jagdschule Werneuchen (Fighter Pilot Training School)

Bf 109s and Fw 190s of JG 2 and JG 26, accompanied by Oberst Galland and Jafü 3 were in a position to thwart all assaults by English bombers and torpedo aircraft. The torpedo aircraft in particular suffered high losses. Battles developed between the Spitfires of Fighter Command and the German fighters and ended to the advantage of the German fighter aircraft. The British reaction to this German operation was surprisingly low key.

During the night of 28/29 March 1942 234 British bombers, some of them already four engined Short Stirlings, the remainder Vickers Wellingtons carried out the first area bombing attack on Lübeck. 304 tons of bombs were dropped. The town centre was virtually destroyed, many in incendiary bombs. 1,425 buildings were totally destroyed; 1,976 severely damaged. 320 civilians were killed and 785 severely injured civilians dragged from the ruins.

Night fighters succeeded in shooting down 12 of the attackers. It was a first taste of what was to come later. Luftwaffe losses for the period 22 June 1941 to 8 February 1942 speak for themselves: 2,951 aircraft totally written-off, in addition, 1,997 damaged and out of service for some time. In the first three months 184 Bf 109s were lost on the eastern front – ie. a quarter of the total.

The year 1942 was to become a year of destiny for the German Reich. Hitler had plans for new offensives but would the strength of the German armed forces be adequate? Since Pearl Harbour (7 December 1941) the United States of America was also involved in the war. What would happen when the American armament industry really got going? In the General Staff of the Luftwaffe and in the German aircraft industry people knew only too well what lay ahead.

7. 1942: Still No New Single Seat Fighter From the Bf 109 F to the Bf 109 G

One letter was to have increasingly fateful consequences for German airpower. That was the letter written on February 3 1940 by Göring, in his capacity as Commissioner for the Four Year Plan, to Walter Funk, Reichsminister for Industry. Included in this letter were the words: "All armaments plans which can be completed during 1940 or by the spring of 1941 must be promoted with all means at our disposal. All other programmes which would have been completed later must be terminated on industrial capacity grounds in the interests of the above aim." So far as the Bf 109 was concerned Göring had put a stop to all development work and that meant no development of a successor. At that time it was calculated that it took about two years from prototype to series production. Assuming that to be correct, any new aircraft and engines would have had to exist in prototype form in 1941 to be produced in series by 1943. Once the United States joined the war it had to be assumed that they would intervene in the European theatre by 1943 at the latest. Consequently, any successor to the Bf 109 would need the green light for preparation for series production by autumn 1941 at the latest. That did not happen. The German Military Command still believed in the summer of 1941 that no new aircraft types were necessary. Generaloberst Hal-

der, Chief of General Staff of the army, declared on July 9 1941 that he regarded the eastern campaign as already decided. Secretary of State, Generalfeldmarschall Erhard Milch declared to representatives of the aircraft industry who were applying for allocation of raw materials for development work, that the war in the east had already been decided. If aircraft really were needed then the existing designs could be improved and so save the cost of developing new types. In this instance Hitler was somewhat more far-sighted than his Generals. In a directive to the armaments industry dated July 14 1941 he ordered that armament work be concentrated on the construction of submarines and aircraft. But he too added the comment that the army needed no fresh equipment as the Russian campaign was already decided.

What was the situation with new fighters? Apart from the Fw 190 there was nothing. The first series Fw 109 A-1, which still had engine problems, was delivered to Jagdgeschwader 2 and 26 in the west between October 1941 and April 1942. Front line experience with the aircraft showed that it was in need of further development. The Fw 190 had a baptism of fire: it was involved in operation "Donnerkeil" (codename of the German navy operation which managed the breakthrough of battle cruisers up the

Above: Bf 109 F-4 B of 10. (Jabo)/JG 26. Below: Same type of I./JG 54 in the Winter of 1941/42

Above: Me 309 V-1 nearing completion. Below: The twin fuselage Klemm K1 25 as a test-vehicle for the Bf 109 Z

English Channel).

It turned out later that the shortcomings of the BMW 801 engine at altitudes of above 20,000 feet meant that the majority of the Fw 190s produced were used for ground attack. Consequently there was not likely to be any serious reduction in the need for a new fighter. The Bf 109F was the best version of the Bf 109 but it was beginning to lose performance through the installation of heavier armament. The Bf 109 F-4B fighter bomber version could carry a bomb load equivalent to the E-4B, the F-4 *trop.* a load equivalent to the E-4N *trop.* Experiments in the field with MG 151/15s mounted under the wings of a Bf 109 F-4/R6 caused such a reduction in performance through additional weight and increased drag that the experiments were abandoned.

The photo reconnaissance Bf 109 F-5 with armament reduced to 2 MG 17s proved to be a particularly useful tool. An Rb 50/30 was installed and to increase its range it was equipped with a 300 litre drop tank release as standard. The F6 was a further development with neither armament nor radio. It had the Rb 50/20/30 or Rb 75/30 photographic equipment. This version had a maximum speed of 373mph. These aircraft tended to be used in the Mediterranean and over Britain. Test flying on Bf 109 V24, V30, V30a and V31 had led to the first prototype of the Me 309 V1, GE + CU and it had its maiden flight on July 18 1942. Three more prototypes were under construction and were completed and tested during 1942. But by the end of 1942 the future of the Me 309 had still not been decided.

In 1941 Messerschmitt was working on another replacement development for the Bf 109, the Me 155. Originally, it was to be a carrier-based aircraft but when the construction of aircraft carriers was halted the Technical Office ordered that it be redesigned as a fighter-bomber. The designs submitted did not meet with approval however. Many changes were demanded. But then someone had the idea that the Me 155 could be turned into a high altitude fighter by increasing the wing area and fitting an exhaust turbocharger. The design was in fact approved but there were delays in placing an order. In 1943 there had still been no order and by then Messerschmitt had neither the design nor the construction capacity available and handed the development over to Blohm & Voss.

At this time there were already proposals for the standardisation of aircraft types – a restriction on types. In the light of this the Messerschmitt organisation became involved in the design of twin fuselage aircraft (as for example the He 111 Z (Zwilling = twin) based on the Bf 109 and the Me 309. To gain experience 2 Klemm Kl 25 light aircraft were put together to form a twin fuselage aircraft and submitted to intensive flight testing which proved satisfactory. These designs had the advantage that a heavy fighter or fighter-bomber of this type needed no new parts (except from the wing centre section) and could be constructed using components taken directly from the assembly line. This applied to the Bf 109 Z. This made the production of test aircraft not only easier but also cheaper. From the above it will be clear that in the middle of 1940 there was still no successor to the Bf 109. The only option was therefore to increase engine power and firepower to improve the performance still further. The DB 605, a development of the DB 601, was available as a new engine and the basic A version produced 1475 PS at take-off.

The DB 605 had been developed specially as a high altitude engine in an attempt to

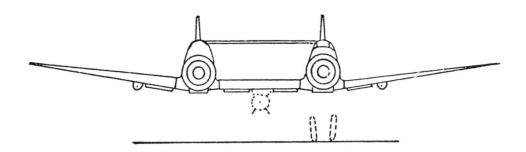

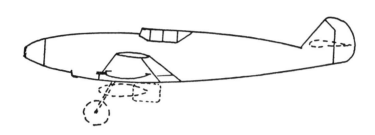

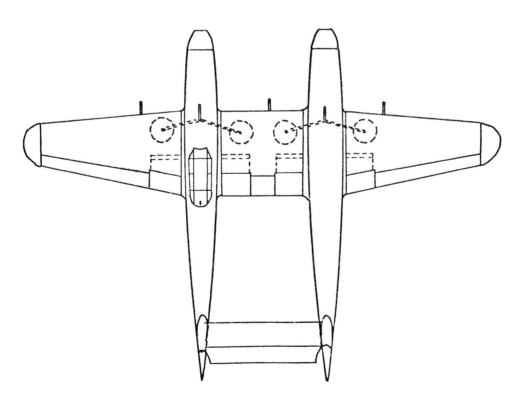

161

General arrangement drawing of project Bf 109 Z

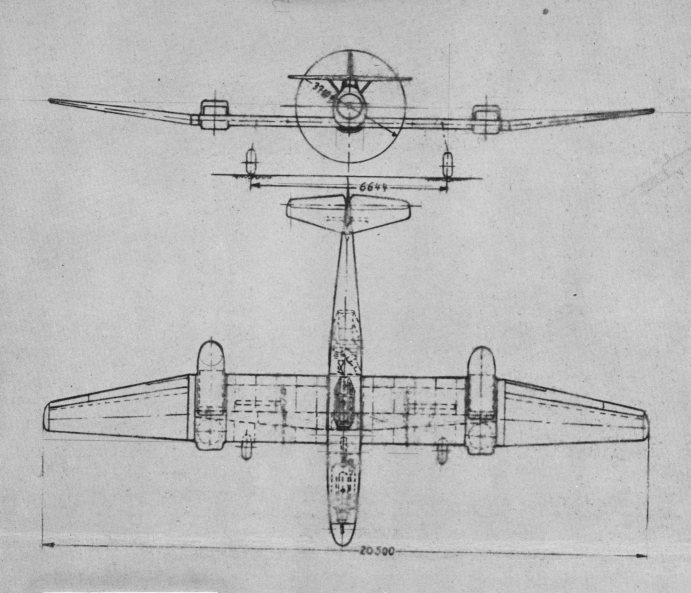

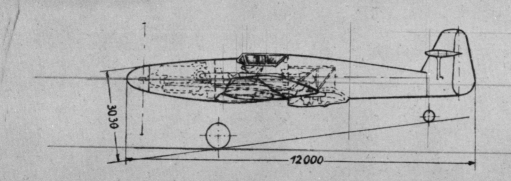

RLM typesheet of Me 155 B1

Winter War on the eastern front 1941/42: Above: Bf 109 F-4 with emergency winter camouflage. Below: Bf 109 F-4 of III./JG 54

This Bf 109 F-4 was captured by the Russians and handed over to the Americans after close inspection.
Below: This same aircraft was flown by the Americans with the registration number EB-1, later EB 100

match the better rate of climb of the Spitfire. The Bf 109 E had an operational altitude of 29,500 ft (ceiling 34,250 ft) and the F 33,000 ft and 37,000 ft respectively. But now there was a need for a fighter aircraft which could engage in combat at 40,000 ft. There were repeated improvements to the DB 605 during production and one of these was the AM version with methanol injection for short term emergency power boost to 1,800 PS. The AJ version using different gearing only produced 1435 PS. The highest power version was the DC which had a higher compression ratio of 8.5:1 and developed 2000 PS. Between 1943 and 1945 various engines were installed in the Bf 109 and produced wide variations in performance. The DB 605 was also used as the power plant for the HZ systems in the Henschel Hs 130 E high altitude aircraft. The DB 605 was built under licence in Sweden and Italy. By combining 2 DB 605s Daimler-Benz developed the DB 610 *Doppellemotor* (2950PS) which was installed in the Ju 288 C and G and also in the He 177 A-3, A-4, A-5, A-6 & A-7, but reliability problems were never solved.

For the time being the armament of the Bf 109 F-4, one MG 151/20 and two MG 17s, was retained. There were however considerable changes to the airframe. It was designed to have a pressurized cockpit but there were also versions with a normal cockpit. The wing design was strengthened, the leading edge flaps now operated on rollers, and pipework was fitted as standard for the installation of the GM-1 system. Rack fittings were incorporated under the fuselage as standard. Other attachment facilities were still being tested. The oil tank had a capacity of 36 litres. Automatic radiator shutters regulated water and oil temperature and the pilot was better protected·

through increased armour plating and the upper cockpit design.

A pre-production series of 12 Bf 109 G-0s was built, but the engine was still the DB 601 E. These aircraft were tested in the field at the beginning of 1942. The tests were satisfactory and a contract was placed for series production of the Bf 109 G-1 equipped with the DB 605 A. Take-off weight had increased dramatically. Whereas the Bf 109 E-1 weighed 2505kg at take-off the Bf 109 G-2 was a disturbing 3200kg.

When the first Bf 109 G-1s were allocated in the middle of 1941 pilots reported that the new Bf 109 was not an improvement but in fact worse than previous versions. On circuit with flaps and undercarriage lowered, full power was needed to prevent it stalling and crashing. There had already been many accidents with the Bf 109 but now the accident rate increased dramatically. Unfortunately there was no two-seater version on which *ab initio* pilots could receive training from the old hands on how to cope with the vices of the Bf 109 "Gustav". The young fighter pilots were trained on B, C, E or F versions and were pitifully accident-prone when trying to cope with the vices of the Bf 109 G. Being a fighter pilot was not easy in the summer of 1942.

On 18th June 1942 Brigadier-General Carl Spaatz had taken command of the 8th US Army Air Force (USAAF) being assembled in Great Britain. On 22 June 1942 Rommel was preparing his new offensive which was to reach Cairo within a week. Generalfeldmarschall Kesselring, Paratroop General Student and the Italian General Staff had all pressed for Operation "Hercules", the landing on Malta, as the highest priority, but Rommel was short of time and wanted to pre-empt the British attack. This was a decision he was to regret bitterly. He had to

Above and left:
Bf 109 F-4 of I./JG 51
on the eastern
front

Opposite: The
Bf 109 F-5 was used
by the
reconnaissance
formations
increasingly. Top:
The Bf 109 F-5 prior
to take-off. Bottom:
After the mission the
exposed film cassette
from the automatic
topographic camera
is taken out

Bf 109 F-5 of Auflkl. Gr. 122

The pilot of this Bf 109 F-4 strayed into Switzerland on July 25 and landed at Belpmoos

Bf 109 F-4 of the Rumanian Air Force

Bf 109 F of the Slovak Fighter Squadron

break off his attack on 3 July. The British and American Chiefs of Staff decided on the North African landings on 24 July. Despite very heavy losses the British succeeded in bringing oil and supplies to Malta between 10 and 13 August. It was no longer possible to take Malta.

On 19 August the British attacked Dieppe with large Royal Air Force formations. The fighter formations at the disposal of Jafü 2 (Oberst Huth) and 3 (Oberst Ibel) were largely Fw 190s though there were also some Bf 109 G-1s. Although numerically inferior they shot down 106 enemy aircraft for the loss of 48 of their own. On the same day the Commander-in-Chief of the 6th Army on the Eastern Front gave the order to attack Stalingrad. On the following day something occurred which Commander-in-Chief of Luftflotte 3, Generalfeldmarschall Sperrle, had been fearing for some time, namely the first attack by the 8th USAAF. They used Boeing B-17 E bombers with about 500 British and American fighters as escort. Amiens, the German supplies crossroads, was the target. The American pilots still lacked confidence but the experienced British fighter pilots prevented any serious losses. The German fighters simply could not penetrate the protective shield of fighter aircraft so the Americans were able to drop their bombs virtually unimpeded but often missed their target. German fighter pilots now knew what to expect in the future.

It had become obvious in the air battles over North Africa that the Bf 109F was technically inferior to the Spitfire and Tomahawk in fire power: they were both armed with two 20mm Hispano cannons whereas the Bf 109 F-4 only had one MG 151/20. When the Bf 109 G-1 was developed a Bf 109 G-1 *trop.* was equipped with two MG 131s (13mm calibre) over the engine instead of the usual MG 17. Because of the larger dimensions of the MG 131 a metal cowling was necessary to fair in the breech mechanism and ammunition feed chute and this gave the Bf 109 G the look which was later seen as typical. Fighter pilots no longer referred to it as the "the Me" or "the Gustav" but to "the Beule" (boil) or "Beulenpest" (the bubonic plague).

One of the first pilots to fly the Bf 109 G-1 *trop.* was Hans-Joachim Marseille who had in the meantime been promoted to the rank of Hauptmann.

On 31 August 1942 Rommel tried once again to break through the British lines at El Alamein. Two days later his attempt failed.

Generalfeldmarschall Kesselring wanted to have one last attempt to defeat Malta from the air. With this in mind the whole of the JG 53 (sections of which had been transferred to the Eastern Front) and I./JG 77 were assembled with the fighter groups. The beginning of the renewed air offensive was set for 10 October 1942. It would appear from available reports from the High Command of the Luftwaffe that at this point the Luftwaffe had reached its greatest numerical strength yet. The figures for fighter planes were as follows:

Works drawing of Bf 109 G-1 ➤

170

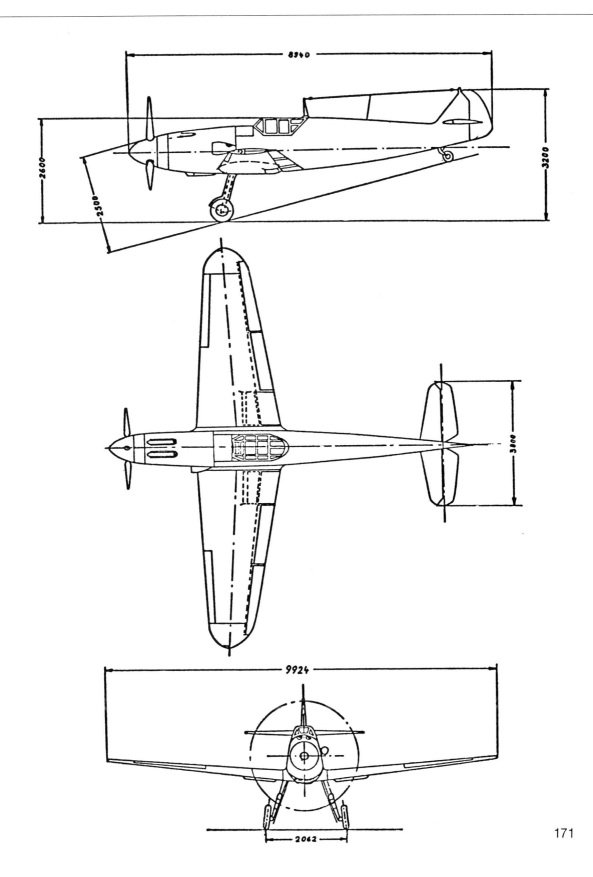

8940

3200

2600

2500

3000

9924

2062

171

Series construction of the Bf 109 G in Augsburg

Right: Instrument panel of the Bf 109 G

Opposite: One of the first prototypes of the G series was
Bf 109 G-0, CC + PO

Luftwaffe Fighter Formations (as at 20.9.1942)

Formation		Bf 109	Fw 190
Eastern Front		Numbers in brackets represent number of aircraft actually serviceable	
2. (H) Staffel Aufkl. Reconnaissance)	Gr. 21	7 (5)	
3. St. Aufkl. Ob.d.L.		2 (2)	
II. Gruppe	JG 3	37 (32)	
Stab	JG 51	– (5)	
I. Gruppe	JG 51		41 (35)
II. Gruppe	JG 51	33 (25)	
III. Gruppe	JG 51	35 (18)	
IV. Gruppe	JG 51	32 (21)	
15. Staffel	JG 51 (Spanish)	11 (7)	
Stab	JG 54	4 (4)	
I. Gruppe	JG 54	34 (25)	
II. Gruppe	JG 54	32 (30)	
III. Gruppe	JG 54	30 (29)	
Stab	JG 77	6 (6)	
5. and 6. Staffel	JG 77	16 (10)	
III. Gruppe	JG 77	33 (24)	
Total on the Eastern Front		317 (243)	41 (35)

Mediterranean and Africa

Formation		Bf 109	Fw 190
4. (H) Staffel Aufkl. Reconnaissance)	Gr. 12	4 (3)	
Stab	JG 27	3 (2)	
I. Gruppe	JG 27	28 (15)	
II. Gruppe	JG 27	26 (16)	
III. Gruppe	JG 27	28 (18)	
Jabo-Staffel Afrika (fighter-bomber)		27 (14)	
III. Gruppe	JG 53	27 (14)	
III. Gruppe	ZG 1	27 (18)	
I. (F) Staffel Aufkl.	Gr. 122	3 (2)	
Stab	JG 53	5 (5)	

		Bf 109		Fw 190	
II. Gruppe	JG 53	32	(25)		
I. Gruppe	JG 77	34	(24)		
Jagdkommando 27		11	(6)		

		Bf 109		Fw 190	
Total		255	(162)		

Western Front

		Bf 109		Fw 190	
1. (F) Staffel Aufkl. (Reconnaissance)	Gr. 33	4	(4)		
1. (F) Staffel Aufkl.	Gr. 123	4	(4)	2	(1)
3. (F) Staffel Aufkl.	Gr. 123	4	(3)		
Stab	JG 2			8	(5)
I. Gruppe	JG 2			42	(35)
II. Gruppe	JG 2			40	(35)
III. Gruppe	JG 2			41	(33)
10. Staffel	JG 2			15	(9)
11. Staffel	JG 2	19	(13)		
Stab	JG 26			5	(4)
I. Gruppe	JG 26			39	(32)
II. Gruppe	JG 26			44	(43)
III. Gruppe	JG 26	15	(13)	43	(35)
10. Staffel	JG 26			16	(11)
11. Staffel	JG 26			14	(10)
Stab	1. Jagd-Div.	1	(0)		
Stab	3. Jagd-Div.	1	(1)		

		Bf 109		Fw 190	
Total		48	(38)	309	(253)

Southeast Area

		Bf 109		Fw 190	
Stab	JG 3	3	(2)		
III. Gruppe	JG 3	31	(10)		
I. Gruppe	JG 4	11	(7)		
Stab	JG 52	6	(6)		
I. Gruppe	JG 52	26	(18)		
II. Gruppe	JG 52	41	(36)		

		Bf 109	Fw 190
III. Gruppe	JG 52	48 (35)	
15. Staffel	JG 52 (Croatia)	13 (13)	
I. Gruppe	JG 53	34 (14)	
Total		213 (141)	

Norway

		Bf 109	Fw 190
I. Gruppe	JG 5	35 (28)	
IV. Gruppe (part)	JG 5	3 (3)	
Total		38 (31)	

Arctic Front, Lapland

		Bf 109	Fw 190
Stab	JG 5	2 (1)	
II. Gruppe	JG 5	32 (21)	
9. Staffel	JG 5	10 (10)	
Total		44 (32)	

Home Defence

		Bf 109	Fw 190
Stab	JG 1		2 (2)
I. Gruppe	JG 1	67 (53)	
II. Gruppe	JG 1		60 (19)
III. Gruppe	JG 1		37 (31)
IV. Gruppe	JG 1	37 (14)	30 (10)
Total		104 (67)	129 (62)

These figures can be summarised as follows:

	Bf 109	Fw 190
Soviet Union (Central, North)	317 (243)	41 (35)
Mediterranean, Africa	255 (162)	– –
West	48 (38)	309 (253)
Southeast (Soviet Union, Balkans)	213 (141)	– –
Norway	– –	38 (31)
Arctic, Lapland	44 (32)	– –
Home Defence	104 (67)	129 (62)
Total	981 (683)	517 (381)

Fw 190s serving with ground attack groups have not been included in this list. Adding both types of fighter produced 1498 single seat fighters theoretically available of which only 1064 were completely serviceable. The rest were being repaired or were unserviceable through lack of spares or engines. That means that a good third of the single seat fighters were not serviceable and in total there were only approximately 1000 single seat fighters available to defend the airspace above the army and across the whole of the German Reich including occupied countries. It never became possible to increase these fighter numbers significantly. In 1941 and in the first half of 1942 approximately 4000 Bf 109s were built but only approximately 1000 remained. This shows how high fighter losses must have been during that period. The figures for the Fw 190 are not quite so bad. In 1941 and during the first half of 1942 approximately 1100 Fw 190s were built and there were still about 500 left, loss rate of over 50%.

If we assume the Eastern Front to be approximately 3700 miles long and that to defend it there were now exactly 361 fighters available, of which only 278 were serviceable, it means that there was one serviceable fighter aircraft per 13 miles. Bearing in mind that the 8th USAAF was able to provide 500 escort fighters for the attack on Amiens and that Luftflotte 3 in the West and the Luftwaffe Commander-in-Chief of the German Reich had only 590 fighters between them, of which only 420 were serviceable, one can't fail to wonder how the Luftwaffe Command imagined that they would defend European airspace. Doubt has often been cast, both in Germany and in other countries, on the number of kills claimed by German fighter pilots. They are however a simple fact. The German fighter pilots had no option but to attack and shoot down other aircraft without regard for their own losses. When the enemy has at least ten times as many aircraft there is no shortage of targets. With so few German aircraft in the skies it would have been difficult for opposing fighter pilots to achieve a similar number of kills.

The Bf 109 G had already been deployed

in the West and in the Mediterranean. In the Summer of 1942 it also saw service on the Eastern Front. It had a dual role. Hermann Graf of 9./JG 52, who had just achieved his 111th victory, wrote in his diary on 10 July 1942: "We are due to get new Me 109s from Germany, the G series. In the squadron they have been complaining about it. They said it was a poor aircraft, the engine was no good and so on: my squadron would be the first to find out for themselves. So we went back to Charkov to exchange aircraft. On my very first flight I was enthusiastic about the aircraft. It was much better than the Me 109 F."

About this time a new fighter appeared on the other side, which was initially mistaken for the Fw 190, often with unfortunate consequences. It was the Lavochkin La 5. The Battle of Stalingrad was in its early stages. After the Soviet victory the La 5 was christened the "wooden guardian angel of Stalingrad".

Was the G ("Gustav") series 109 really as bad as has often been claimed?

Major Gollob, Kommodore of JG 77, had just gained his 150th victory in the air in August, flying the "Gustav". Graf, at that time still Staffelkapitän (Officer Commanding) 9./JG 52, had 140 victories and he too was already flying the Bf 109 G. It was probably rather like the difference between the Fokker DVII and DVIII in 1918. In the hands of an experienced pilot the Fokker DVIII was an excellent aircraft but inexperienced pilots did tend to "prang" it. Anybody could fly the Fokker DVII. In the hands of experienced pilots the Bf 109 G was a good weapon although it was definitely a problem for the young pilots with minimum training. But they had to fly it, there was nothing else. Hermann Graf showed what an old hand could do with the "Gustav" on 3 September

1942 near Stalingrad. His wingman had lost contact and he found himself alone against almost 20 Yak 1s. In a hard-fought dogfight Graf not only escaped but achieved his 145th kill by shooting down a Yak 1.

The new air offensive against Malta was going wrong. The British had had time to transfer more Spitfires to Malta. The German Bf 109s, the Italian Macchi MC 202s and Reggiane Re 2001s could not prevent Spitfires from Malta attacking the KG 54, 30, 60 and 77 bombers which suffered heavy losses. It was no longer possible to use Stukas at all . . . 105 Bf 109s were lost.

On 23 October the British 8th Army under Montgomery attacked El Alamein with the support of approximately 880 aircraft. The weak German fighter formations, Stab, II. and III./JG 27 and III./JG 53 did not stand a chance against the British fighter formations which outnumbered them many times over. In addition there was a shortage of fuel which meant that many pilots could not take off and had to escape as best they could from the British troops flooding across the German-Italian front lines.

Kesselring used I./JG 27, I./JG 77 and III./JG 77 for defence. But it was too late. In spite of Hitler's telegram "Hold your ground at any cost!" Rommel gave the order to retreat on 4 November. It was in the context of this retreat that I./JG 77 under Hauptmann Heinz Bär had its first major success in Africa. It was flying as an escort to a group of Stukas which was attacked by South African Hurricanes. The 109s defeated the squadron totally. Six Hurricanes were shot down and of the remainder there was not a single aircraft left undamaged. But it was to no avail for on the night of 8 November 1942 the Allies landed behind the German and Italian troops in Algeria and Morocco. That was the beginning of the end for the Afrika-Korps.

Wiener Neustädter Flugzeugwerke (WNF) built the Bf 109 under licence. Above left: Deep drawing press. Above right: Fuselage construction. Below: Production of components

Although unbeaten in the air, Hans-Joachim Marseille was killed on September 30th, 1942 when his Bf 109 G-2 *trop.*, "Gelben 14" (Yellow 14) crashed

The "Star of Africa" Hans-Joachim Marseille, who was still unbeaten in combat, was killed in an air crash on 30 September 1942 when flying his "Gelbe 14".

On 19 November the Russians launched their major attack on the Don with the aim of trapping the German 6th Army under Generaloberst Paulus (which was concentrated around Stalingrad) and destroying it. The tragedy of Stalingrad took its course.

Kesselring reacted to the Allied landings in Algeria and Morocco extremely quickly. Paratroopers took control of the airfield at El Aouina in Tunisia. On 14 November 1942 II./JG 51 returned from Russia with their Bf 109 Gs. They were followed by II./JG 2 from France with their Fw 190s, the first of this type to appear in the Mediterranean theatre. II./JG 53 was also transferred to Tunisia and III./JG 53 went to Sicily. There was now a slight numerical superiority of German/Italian aircraft in Tunisia. But in qualitative terms there was no doubt that the Allies had a clear advantage in the air. Fuel supply problems grew worse. On 2 November Benghazi was taken by the British. On 5 December II./JG 77 came to Libya so that the whole of JG 77, now under Major Müncheberg, (who had already been in Africa as Oberleutnant and Staffelkapitän of JG 26) was now assembled in Africa. On the previous day 60 German fighter aircraft, Bf 109s and Fw 190s, had totally destroyed a British Bisley bomber squadron with Spitfire escorts. The end of the year saw the 6th Army virtually annihilated in the East and the Germans steadily retreating in the Mediterannean. What lay ahead in 1943?

Marseille before one of his last sorties in the "Gelben 14"

Another Bf 109 G-2 *trop.* of I./JG 27 in Libya, summer 1942
Bf 109 G-1/R6 of III./JG 77 in Russia 1942. In front of it Feldwebel Furth and Pichler. The wolf's head, the Gruppe emblem is clearly visible

8. Fighting to the bitter end in Stalingrad and Africa
The Bf 109 G becomes a Maid-of-all-Work

The end of 1942 and the beginning of 1943 were dominated by increasingly heavy night air raids on Germany by Royal Air Force Bomber Command. The tragedy of Stalingrad ended on 2 February 1943 when the last few soldiers still fit to fight were forced to surrender.

On 6 March Rommel again attempted an offensive from Mareth. Once more Müncheberg's JG 77 Bf 109 Gs had a good day. On 26 February Curtiss Kittyhawks of the Western Desert Air Force, mainly New Zealanders and South Africans, made a low-level attack on German positions in the Mareth line and JG 77 engaged in heavy fighting and shot down 16 of the attackers; at least the same number returned with considerable damage. Then something happened which was to have very serious consequences. The British brought the new Spitfire IX to the Front and it was superior in all respects to the Bf 109 G. Unfortunately it was just at this time that the II./JG 2 with Fw 190 A-5s was withdrawn from the Mediterranean theatre. On 23 March "Jochen" Müncheberg was killed in action over Tunisia. He was laid to rest in El Aouina. Subsequently operations in Africa soon came to an end. On 12 and 13 May 1943 the remainder of the "Heeresgruppe Afrika" under Generaloberst von Arnim capitulated after Rommel had to give up his command for health reasons.

In Russia heavy defensive battles were fought along the whole front. "Vorwärts, Kameraden, wir müssen zurück!" ("Forward, comrades, we must retreat!") was a favourite joke on the Eastern Front. But still the Eastern Front held. A new offensive at Kursk was prepared.

That was the first half of 1943.

Meanwhile Messerschmitt had been attempting not only to improve the Bf 109 G but also to make it more adaptable. Just as with the Fw 190, it was to be used for short range reconnaissance, long range reconnaissance, bombing, ground attack, combat against bombers and fighters, in short to do everything that the bombers (whose production had been increasingly cut back), could no longer do.

Field modification kits and conversion kits were used to produce fresh variants of what was actually an outdated design. The suffix 'U' (Umrüst-Bausatz) indicates modification kit, and 'R' (Rüstsatz) field modification kit (add-on assembly). The following field modification kits are known to have existed:

U1: Messerschmitt P6 device to reverse propeller pitch for shorter landings.

U2: Wooden tailplane.

U3: MW50 (Methanol/Water) injection unit for short-term emergency power boost.

U4: Wooden tailplane together with semi-retractible tail wheel.

U6: Improved version of U4.

R1: ETC 500/IXb rack under the fuselage.

R2: ETC 50/VIIId bomb rack for four SC 50 bombs.

R3: Rack for 300 litre drop tank.

R4: 300 litre drop tank rack under each wing, available faired and unfaired.

R5: MK 108 (30mm calibre) under each wing, faired in.

R6: Similar installation of two MG 151/20s.

R7: Rearward warning system.

The modification kits could only be installed by the manufacturer or in a repair workshop but the field modification kits were stored at Luftzeugamt Erding and from there were ordered by Geräte-Ausgabe-Stellen, (GAST) by the air parks and the maintenance units where installation took place. Although the Bf 109 G-1 was designed with a pressurized cockpit the need for increased production output caused Messerschmitt to build a simplified version without one. This was the Bf 109 G-2 which was the same as the G-1 in other respects. Engine supplies left much to be desired. Messerschmitt could not obtain delivery of the DB 605 in the quantities he required. There were however considerable numbers of DB 601 A-1s available so, making a virtue out of necessity, it was decided to build a Bf 109 G-3 incorporating a pressurized cabin but powered by the DB 601 A-1. The G-1, G-2 and G-3 had identical armament. But the G-3 had a modernised radio unit, being fitted with the FuG 16Z instead of the previous FuG 7A. This equipment was supplied by the firm of Lorenz and together with the FuG 10 was used to lead fighter formations.

The "Black Men", the formation ground crews had to keep the aircraft ready for service at any time and in all types of weather. Here seen with III./JG 52 in Russia

Opposite: As early as 1942 the number of serviceable aircraft was reducing continuously. Above: Bf 109 G-2 *trop.*

Below: G-4 of III./JG 3. Yellow ring round the fuselage was used for a time for all aircraft deployed on the eastern front

Similar to the Bf 109 F-5 was the Bf 109 G-4 fighter-reconnaissance aircraft produced in 1943. Whereas the F-5 had been without cannon, the G-4 had the full fighter armament of two MG-17s and an MG 151/20. This reconnaissance version did not have a pressurized cabin.

Bf 109 G-2 without visible markings on the eastern front 1942

Bf 109 G-3/R6 with unusual winter camouflage

Photos from the other side of the lines: Top: Bf 109 G-2 which made a forced landing behind Soviet lines. Centre: Russian experts inspect a captured Bf 109 G-2 Bottom: A Bf 109 G-2 captured by the Russians, bearing Soviet markings

187

The numerical inferiority of the German fighters was particularly noticeable in the northern section of the eastern front. Above: Victory laurel wreath for this pilot of 8./JG 5 who had just made the 100th kill. Below: The most successful Finnish fighter pilot, Lt. Lunkkanen with Oberleutenant Götz and a Bf 109 G-2 of I./JG 54

Germany still had support: Above: Hungarian Bf 109 G-2 *trop*. Below: Bf 109 F-4 of the Finnish Air Force

Above: A Bf 109 G-2 delivered to Switzerland. Below: Bf 109 G-2 *trop.* **Works no. 10639, Royal Air Force no. RN 288 was investigated at Collyweston on 26 December 1943 and test flown on 8 February 1944**

Re-equipping the short-range reconnaissance formations with Bf 109 fighter reconnaissance aircraft began in 1943. The Henschel Hs 126 which had still been in use in 1941 on the Eastern Front and in Africa had been replaced by the Fw 189 to a large extent, and, because of its low speed, could now only be used on the Eastern Front. On the Western Front and in the Mediterranean the fighter-reconnaissance versions of the Bf 109 F were in use. Only a short series of the Bf 109 G-4 was built but its successor the Bf 109 G-8 became the standard short-range reconnaissance aircraft. Originally these units in the form of reconnaissance squadrons 'H' were part of reconnaissance groups. From the beginning of the war these had each consisted of an 'F' reconnaissance squadron for long range reconnaissance (F = Fernaufklärung) and an 'H' reconnaissance squadron (H = Heer) – the battle reconnaissance squadron of the Korps and Panzer divisions of the Heer, the army. The 'F' squadrons normally consisted of 12 aircraft whereas the 'H' squadrons consisted of 12 short-range reconnaissance aircraft and 3 liaison aircraft. Changing over to Bf 109 fighter reconnaissance aircraft in 1943 to change from the Fw 189, usually to the Bf 109 G-4 and later the G-8. The activities of the Russian Air Force were becoming a serious threat to German reconnaissance aircraft, and to a lesser extent to the Fw 190 A-3/U4 and A-5/U4, resulted in reorganisation: from now on long-range reconnaissance groups and short-range reconnaissance groups were formed. The latter generally had two squadrons but some had three. On the Eastern Front too it was necessary in 1943 to change from the Fw 189, usually to the Bf 109-G-4 and later the G-8. The activities of the Russian Air Force were becoming a serious threat to

German reconnaissance aircraft in 1943. Reconnaissance pilots confirmed that Russian fighter resistance against them strengthened increasingly from 1943 onwards.

Subsequent to the Bf 109 G-4 reconnaissance fighter, Messerschmitt produced the G-5 which looked rather different. It had the armament of the Bf 109 G-1 *trop:* two MG 131s and one MG 151/20. This gave it what had now become the typical Bf 109 'bulge' from this series the MG 17 was no longer mounted above the engine, but only the MG 131 and later also the MG 151.

One of the Bf 109 licensed constructors, the Fieseler Works in Kassel, had been trying for some time to develop the Bf 109 into a fighter bomber with increased wing span similar to the Fw 190 G series. Fieseler did the design work and Skoda in Bohemia & Moravia built this version. As far as it is possible to tell from existing documentation this aircraft designated FiSk 199 (Fieseler/Skoda) looked similar to the Fw 190 D-9 or the Ta 152. There is no record that a test aircraft was built, but a Bf 109 G-0, BD + GC, was converted to test development potential. The DB 601 was replaced by a DB 605 A-1. Two R4 drop tanks and an ETC 500 stores rack was added. As the aircraft was to carry an SC 500 bomb or a jettisonable stores container of the same weight, the aircraft was fitted with a replaceable third wheel, which plugged in at a point beneath the back of the pilot's seat and was designed to be jettisoned after take-off.

In the meantime a Bf 109 G-5 underwent a fundamental transformation. Messerschmitt was still determined to produce a successor to the Bf 109. Although tests of the Me 309 were going ahead he favoured something more like the long-nosed Fw 109 D-9. And he had also become aware of the

The Bf 109 G-0,
BD+GC was used as
a test-vehicle for the
planned FiSk 199
Above left: The third
wheel was jettisoned
after take-off

Fw 190 V-30/U1. This aircraft, which led to the Ta 152 H, had excellent performance, especially at altitude. So it was decided to build a new Me 209. As new designs were still not being approved, this aircraft was developed under the designation Me 209 V5 — although it didn't have the slightest connection with the Me 209! The engine needed for it, the DB 603, was not available immediately so construction was delayed until November 1943.

Another Bf 109 development project had suffered a serious setback in 1943. The prototype of the Bf 109 Z, NG + RS, was severely damaged during a British night air raid on Augsburg before it had even flown. It was a heavy fighter made by combining two Bf 109 F-4s. Later it was decided to save time by using the Bf 109 G. Before the prototype could be reconstructed the RLM decided to combine the development of Bf 109 Z with that of the Me 309 and this combined design was known as the Me 609. Neither of these projects saw completion.

At the end of January, Messerschmitt looked into the possibility of converting the Bf 109 to accept jet engines. It was debatable whether it was worth justifying the Me 309 at the expense of a Bf 109 with a new DB 603 engine. It was at this time that the feasibility of series production of the Me262 jet fighter was examined. In the light of the standardisation policy, which restricted production to a few designs, it was necessary to check whether the production of 130 Me 262s was compatible with the requirement of the Technisches Amt for short term delivery. This investigation led to the decision to proceed with the production of the 130 Me 262s.

A jet propulsion conversion for the Bf 109 or preferably the Me 155 (which at the request of the RLM had been changed time and time again at the design stage), was certainly possible. Performance would be equivalent to that of the Me 262 or perhaps even better. The armament could be the same. The difficulty lay in the fact that jet engines mounted under the wings would require a totally different undercarriage arrangement. A jet fighter of this sort would be only a temporary solution. In any case the development of the Me 262 had already progressed so far that redesigning the Me 155 would have delayed the development of jet aircraft. So this project was filed away although a suitable design was available.

In the meantime the Allies had been active. Churchill, Roosevelt and the British and American Staffs had decided on a combined bomber offensive against Germany and this began on 10 June 1943. American bomber formations were to bomb targets during the day and the RAF area bombing raids were to be carried out at night. The raids were to be targeted on German fighter bases and factories.

From this moment on the German Reich was battered day and night. The British began with a raid on Düsseldorf with almost 700 bombers on the night of 11/12 June 1943. Flak and night fighters succeeded in shooting down 38 of the bombers. The next night it was Bochum's turn. This time 24 out of 454 raiders were shot down. On the next day the 8th USAAF bombed Kiel and Bremen. But at this stage the British were still the major force in the bombing raids.

By scraping the barrel it had been possible to combine 1800 aircraft for a renewed German major offensive on the Eastern Front. These aircraft were in Luftflotte 4 (Generaloberst Deßloch) and Luftflotte 6 (Generaloberst Ritter von Greim). But there were only two fighter groups, JG 3

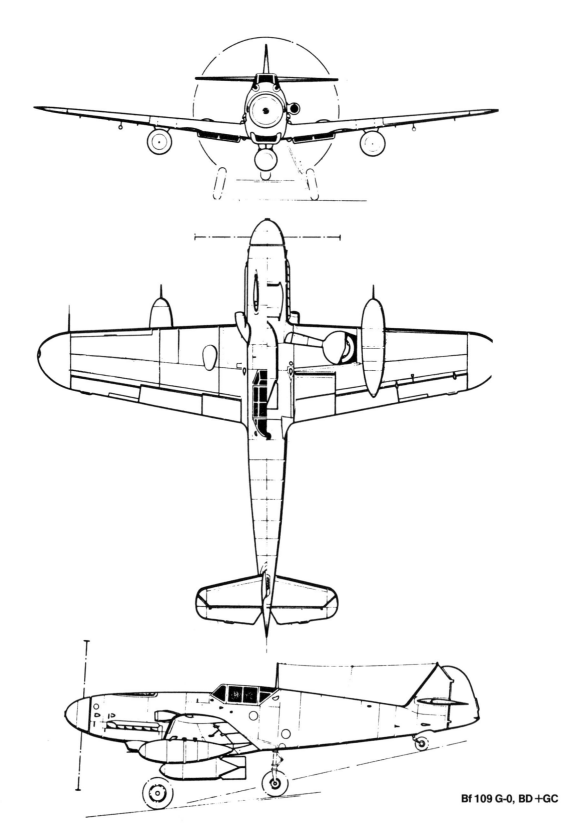

194

Bf 109 G-0, BD + GC

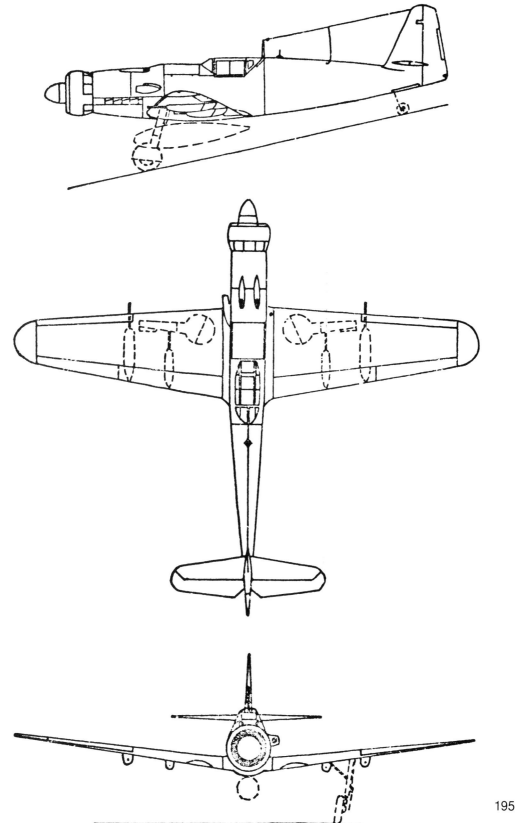

Me 209 V 5

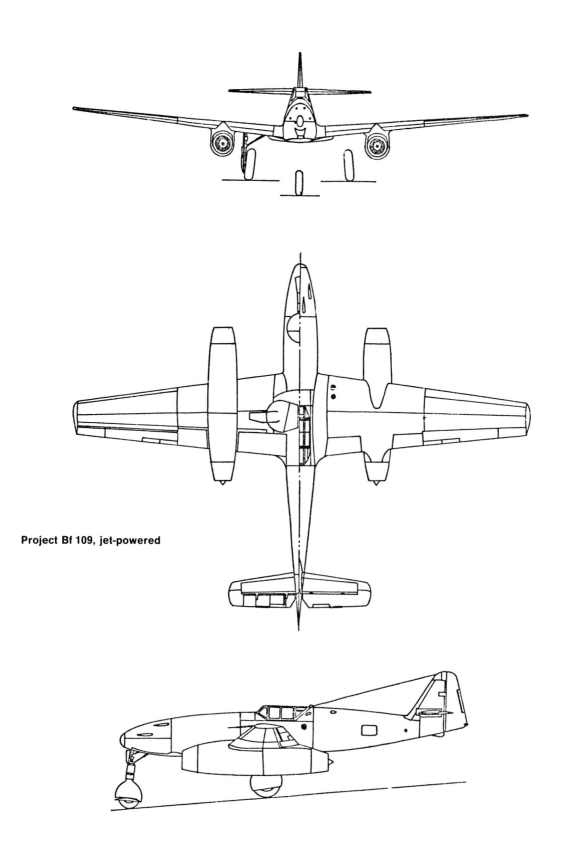

Project Bf 109, jet-powered

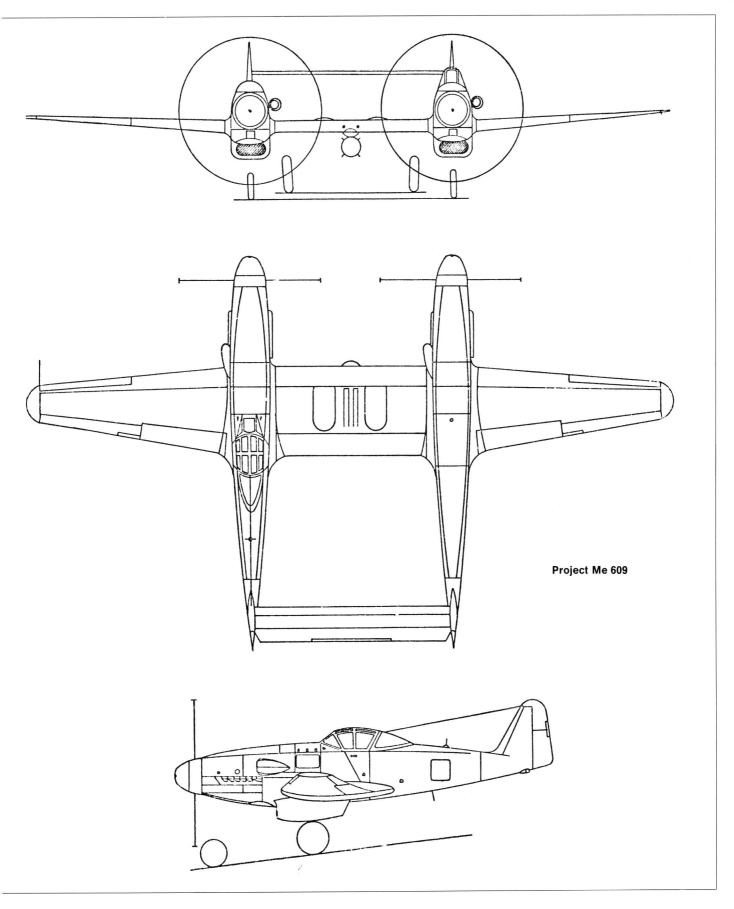

Project Me 609

Me 209 V5 (above). Comparison with the photograph below reveals that Messerschmitt was influenced by Tank's Ta 152 H-0 design

Bf 109 G undergoing maintenance. The barrel of the MG 151/20 is clearly recognisable

and JG 52 (both equipped with the Bf 109 G) which were responsible for controlling air space over the fighting army . . .

Hitler fixed the date for the start of this operation, code-named "Zitadelle" (Citadel), for 5 July 1943. It was to be the last German offensive on the Eastern Front.

JG 54 on the eastern front. Above: Bf 109 G-2 of III. Gruppe. Below: Bf 109 G-2 of II.Gruppe. Mud was a problem on the airfields

Photographs of the same units. "Grünherz" (Green Heart) Squadron emblem. Above: II.Gruppe "Löwe von Aspern" (Lion of Aspern). Below: III.Gruppe.

9. Retreat on all Fronts
Mass production of Bf 109 G-6

In the spring of 1943 deliveries of the new Bf 109 G-6 began but it was only in the Summer of that year that the last G-2s, G-3s and G-5s were delivered. The G-6 was to become the standard Luftwaffe fighter. Fw 190 A-5s predominated in the West, while the Bf 109 was more common in the East, although here some fighter wings were already flying the Fw 190.

The Bf 109 G-6 was based on the G-5 but had a new increased area tailplane which for part of the production run was made of wood. The fuselage consisted of two metal halves and the wings were one piece single-spar metal construction with slotted ailerons and flaps. There were two flat radiators on the underside of the wing either side of the fuselage which used the boundary layer effect. Airflow exit was controlled by thermostatically operated double 'flaps', the lower part of which extended the main flap towards the fuselage. The other part formed a vent in the skin of the upper wing and opened automatically as soon as the lower one closed. The G-6 had a simple cantilever tailplane, with tailplane and fin of metal and fabric-covered rudder and elevator. All the controls were balanced. When aluminium became scarce towards the end of the war, wooden tailplanes were manufactured in Central Germany in furniture factories. The only

difference in the undercarriage compared with earlier models was that the tailwheel could now be partially or completely retracted. The power plant was the DB 605A, DB 605AS, DB 605ASB, DB 605AM or the DB 605D with various additions for emergency power boost and electrically controlled VDM (Vereinigte Deutsche Metallwerke of Frankfurt-Heddernheim) three-blade variable pitch propellers. The 400 litre fuel tank had been made semi-bulletproof with laminated rubber and was encased in plywood behind and below the pilot's seat. In addition a 300 litre drop tank could be carried under the fuselage. The armament consisted of two MG 131s (13mm calibre) and an MK 108 motor cannon (30mm calibre). The MK 108 had been developed by Rheinmetall-Borsig from 1940 onwards at their own risk in the absence of an RLM contract but in the full knowledge that it would take heavier weapons than were then available to shoot down the four-engined bombers (Stirling, Halifax) which were on the production line in Britain. In 1941 the weapon was demonstrated to Udet who was at that time Generalluftzeugmeister and his words were: "We don't need any aircraft weapons of larger calibre than 20mm to deliver our deadly back-of-the-neck shots" (he meant an attack from above and behind) "to the heaviest bombers, from a range of 20

Above: Steinhoff, later to become Inspecteur der Bundesluftwaffe, flew the Bf 109 in JG 52. He made 149 kills on the eastern front. Below: Capt. Alex Seibanescu, Rumania, achieved most of his victories flying this Bf 109 G-4/R1

Bf 109 G-4 *trop.* **in the hangar of an Italian airfield**

Above: Bf 109 G-5 *trop.* of JG 51 in the Mediterranean. Below: Bf 109 G-5/R6 *trop.* also in the same theatre

Drop tanks were necessary because of the short range of the Bf 109. Above: Bf 109 G-2/R3 on the eastern front. Below: Bf 109 G-6/R3 in the Mediterranean (9./JG 27)

JG 5 was known as the "Eismeer-Geschwader" (Arctic Ocean group). Above: A Bf 109 G taking off on a fighter bomber sortie, Petsamo, 1943. Below; Oberfeldwebel Schulz, 8. Staffel, crashed on 21 March 1943

metres if necessary." This was further proof that the men responsible for the technical development of the war in the air were not up to it. They were so trapped in the thinking of the First World War (in which they had performed excellently) that they could no longer keep pace with rapid developments.

Consequently development of the 30mm 'short cannon' was stopped for the time being. It was only after the death of Udet that the Technisches Amt actually placed a contract for the development of this weapon following demands from various formations. It now became apparent that the breech mechanism would have to be considerably simplified. In addition the materials which were available were subject to metal fatigue. Mass production could not be started until the spring of 1944. Till then pilots flying Bf 109 G-6s had to put up with the trials and tribulations of the MK 108. But in fact the pilots were satisfied with this weapon. The weapons experts had calculated that firing an MK 108 from a distance of 500mm required 48 rounds to achieve a 50% probability of shooting down a four-engined bomber, from 1000m 120 rounds and from 1500m 440 rounds. 95% certainty of succes in shooting it down required 88 rounds from 500m, 230 rounds from 1000m and 800 rounds from 1500m. These statisticss are of purely theoretical value as can be seen from the fact that the motor MK 108 of the Bf 109 G-6 only had a 60-round belt. In fact it was more like this: assuming the target to be 500m away, 88 rounds were required to ensure the four direct hits necessary to bring it down. Eight seconds of firing are needed for that. But if the enemy aircraft reacted immediately its evasive action prevented it being shot down. It was very rarely that even the most experienced fighter pilots achieved this theoretical kill

rate. As the fire rate of the MK 108 was 1300 rounds per minute, only a few short bursts of fire were possible. The same applied to the MG 151/20, for which it was calculated that from a distance of 1000m 840 rounds would be necessary for 95% probability of bringing down a four-engined bomber. This weapon used a disintegrating belt with 100 explosive shells. Assuming a fire rate of 720 rounds per minute this weapon too could only be used for very short bursts. The Allied air crews referred to the MK 108 with it compact appearance and monotonous sound as the "pneumatic drill". The American weapons expert Lt.Col. Chinn wrote in a report on the MK 108 to the US Navy: "Fortunately production of the MK 108 and its installation in jet fighters did not begin early enough – but enough B-17 bombers were lost as a result of it in any case."

Some fighter groups such as JG 1 and JG 26 used the R2 kit to enable the 109 to carry the WGr. 21cm mortar. These were grenades which were normally used by the army for smoke screens and were modified to become rockets. It was only after the success of the Fw 190 A-4/R6 on 14 October 1943 near Schweinfurt that the RLM decided to develop an operational rocket from this "workshop job". First a high grade quality of propellant was used in seven 55cm long tubes: the tubes were later improved. Test firing by Abt. E7 of the Luftwaffe Test Establishment at Rechlin produced the following deviation figures when fired from tubes under the wings of a Fw 190:

Range	Vertical Deviation	Lateral Deviation
1000m	+/− 7m	+/− 40m
2000m	+/− 24m	+/− 84m

The accuracy of these rockets was not very good. The Russians were better at it. Over range of 1000m their deviation figures were similar to those of the 21cm rocket but at a range of 2000m the deviation was 50% less, as was confirmed at Rechlin with a captured RS132 fired from a Bf 110.

The fighter pilots found this weapon unpleasant as it spoilt the stability of the Bf 109 and the Fw 190. They called it the "Dödel".

Also in 1943 the Bf 109 G-6/R1 fighter bombers went into service and like the Bf 109 F-4B they carried an SC 250. The R2 kit was rarely fitted except in the version mentioned above. On the other hand the Bf 109 G-6/R3 was very often flown with a 300 litre drop tank.

July 1943 was to become one of the blackest months since Stalingrad. On 5 July the army groups in the South and the Centre assembled at Kursk for an offensive. "Operation Zitadelle" had begun.

The Russians knew all about German strength and also their plans for attack because they had agents in the German OKW, behind the German lines and had carried out intensive air reconnaissance. Shortly after the Germans opened fire approximately 400 Russian bombers took off to attack the overcrowded German bases. The VIII. Fliegerkorps was warned by a Freya radar installation. Aircraft of JG 3 and JG 52 managed to take off in time, 150 Bf 109 G-2, G-3 and G-5s, and also a few G-6s, flew to intercept the attackers. In the Olchvatka-Poniry area north of Kharkov, Gostichev and Yakovlev one of the most extensive air battles in the Russian campaign took place. Approximately 120 Russian bombers and ground attack fighters were shot down, but to no avail. The army units gained no ground worth mentioning. On 10 July the Allies landed on Sicily. On 12 July the Russians attacked Orel. On the following day Hitler had to order the ending of the operations at Kursk. But then came the heaviest blow, namely "Operation Gomorrah"; day and night raids on Hamburg from 24 to 30 July in which the German radar stations on the ground and in the air (night fighters) were rendered useless by dueppling. The bomber formations lost virtually no aircraft and the German defences had been rendered blind.

But soon the Americans in particular were to notice that not everything worked out the way they imagined. At that time the 8th USAAF consisted of 15 bomber groups with about 300 Boeing B-17 'Fortresses' and Consolidated B-24 'Liberators'. They were still short of long range fighters to protect the bombers however. The Republic P-47 'Thunderbolt' could only reach the Belgian/Dutch border or with drop tanks the frontier of the German Reich. But the Commander of the 8th USAAF did not want to wait any longer: the instructions of the Allied Chiefs of Staff had to be carried out. Fighter aircraft factories had to be destroyed. The first target was the AGO establishment at Oschersleben, southeast of Magdeburg, which built the Fw 190 in major series production.

The attack on AGO was supposed to take place during the series of attacks on Hamburg on 28 July. As the Allied fighters could only escort the B-17s as far as Holland at the most, they had to leave the bombers to fly on unprotected beyond there. General Eaker had assumed that the German forces would be so distracted by "Operation Gomorrah" that fighter resistance would not be very strong. How wrong he was!

Oberleutnant Heinz Knoke of the 5th Squadron of JG 11 had had the idea of dropping bombs on the fuselage of the "Möbelwagen" (= furniture vans – radio code for four-engined bombers). A test with an SC 250 with a delayed action fuse was

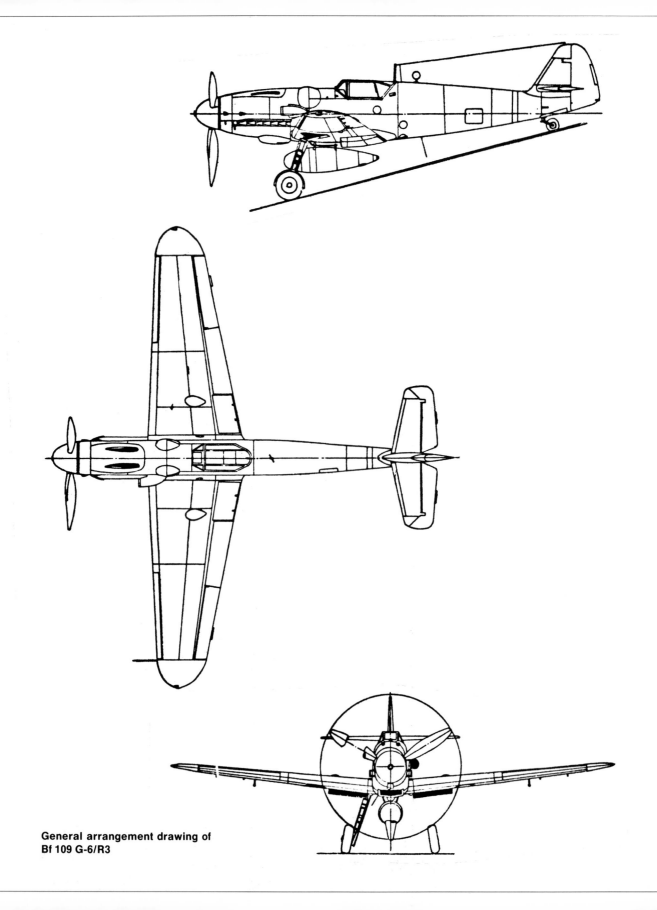

**General arrangement drawing of
Bf 109 G-6/R3**

Lt. Lichtenberg of III./JG 54 (left) and Maj. Nowotny, both killed in 1944 in defence of the Reich.

JG 52, Hauptmann Günter Rall, Oberst Bormann, Kommodore, Maj. Hrabak

Bf 109 G-6 at a fighter training school

I./JG 302 spent some time in Finland. Bf 109 G-6/U2/R6 in Helsinki

Oberlt. ''Bubi''
Hartmann JG 52 in
his Bf 109 G-6

Right: Maintenance of
a Bf 109 G-6 in the
Summer. Below: the
same job in the
Winter

successful. When the American bomber formation arrived it divided into two parts. It was then noticed that the Americans had a second target, namely the Fieseler factories in Kassel. The Fw 190 was being built here too. It is easy to see that the Allies regarded the Fw 190 as being more dangerous than the Bf 109. As soon as ground control in Jever gave the alarm, about 35 Bf 109 G-6s took off. They were the II. group of JG 11. Two squadrons were flying normal Bf 109 G-6s; only the 5th squadron, eleven aircraft, was flying Bf 109 G-6/R1s. The time fuses on the bombs meant that the enemy formation had to be overflown at a particular height separation. The eleven fighter bombers had to estimate this height to avoid failure. But after Feldwebel Fest caused three B-17s to crash with the explosion of just one bomb, the American formation, about 40 B-17s, fell apart and the Bf 109s were now able to engage the aircraft individually. On this one morning II./JG 11 under Hauptmann Specht were able to report that they had shot down eleven B-17s. Of the 77 B-17s which had taken off for Oschersleben and Kassel, 22 did not return. Of the remainder, which returned to British bases, there was not a single machine which had not been damaged by gunfire. Seven German fighters, some Fw 190s, some Bf 109s, were lost. The Americans announced that they had shot down 48 Fw 190s and Bf 109s. That was a slight exaggeration!

Up to "Operation Gomorrah" only the twin-engined heavy fighters (Bf 110 and Ju 88 C) had been used for night fighter work. In February 1943 Major Hermann, a former Bomber Captain, who was at this time technical advisor in the Luftwaffe Operations Staff at Wildpark-Werder, had suggested that in addition to night fighters

The southern sector of the eastern front suffered from extreme heat in the summer. Maintenance on a Bf 109 G

controlled from the ground there should also be independent single-seat night fighters. At that time his proposal was turned down. But now, after the catastrophe of Hamburg, and at the suggestion of Oberst Loßberg, Section Leader in the Technisches Amt, free-ranging night fighter work was introduced and this occasion also saw the offical approval of single-seat fighters being used for night fighter work. As somebody had said that the fighter aircraft should smash into the bomber formations like wild boars, single-seat night fighter work was known colloquially as "Wilde Sau" (= wild boar). Oberst Hermann was made head of the newly set up JG 300 which was to be stationed in Bonn, Rheine and Oldenburg. How thin fighter cover had become by then

Major Eder, JG 26 after a successful sortie

Bf 109 G-6 of Jagdgruppe 50

Major Dahl, Kmdr. III./JG 3 before a sortie

can be seen from the fact that II./JG 300 stationed with II./JG 11 on the airfield at Rheine and III./JG 300 were stationed with II./JG 1 and had to use their Bf 109 Gs during the night. The new fighter pilots were not used to flying single-seaters and generally came back from sorties damaged. This caused the day fighter pilots to hand over no more aircraft or to declare them unserviceable. Generally speaking the "Wilde Sau" policy was successful initially but not in the long run, as we shall see. To begin with "Wilde Sau" was extended. JG 301 was to be stationed in Bavaria, JG 302 in Brandenburg.

Gradually sufficient aircraft became available and all groups of JG 300 flew the Bf 109 G-5/R6 with its new armament of two MG 131 and three MG 151/20. One MG 151/20 was positioned between the cylinders banks of the engine and shot through the hollow propeller spinner whilst the other two were slung under the wings in pods. The Bf 109 G-6 and also the G-4 were used by the Technisches Versuchskommando (Technical Development Group) at Werneuchen to test out radar equiipment such as the FuG 217.

In the meantime on 29 July the 8th USAAF attacked the Arado works and on 30 July the Fieseler works once again. It really did seem as if the Allies did not regard the Bf 109 factories as so important, though in reality it is more likely that the Fw 190 factories were more accessible. The Bf 109 factories were too far east or south, even excluding the Erla factory in Leipzig-Heiterblick on the Mockau airfield, the largest licensed manufacturer of the Bf 109. After the Americans had suffered heavy losses they tried another target. The 9th USAAF stationed in North Africa received orders to attack the oil wells and refineries

in the Ploesti area of Rumania. 178 Consolidated B-24 "Liberators" took off from Benghazi and flew low across the Mediterranean. They had been ordered not to use their radios: the raid was to be a low-level attack to take the defenders by surprise. For the American crews it was to become a very hell. Around the installations, in addition to heavy flak, there were also the much-feared 20mm Vierlinge 38s. When the B-24s came in at no more than 300ft they were greeted with a hail of tracer fire. The Bf 109 Gs of I./JG 4 under Hauptmann Hans Hahn and of IV./JG 27 under Oberleutnant Burk did the rest; in addition there were a few Rumanian Bf 109 G-2s and a few Bf 110 G-2s of IV./NJG 6. The result of the operation was devastating for the Americans: of the 178 B-24s that had taken off, 48 were shot down and over 50 aircraft returned so badly damaged that they were not worth repairing. Not a single B-24 returned undamaged. The damage caused to the Ploesti installations by bombs and incendiaries was repaired in a fairly short time. The losses suffered during this attack and also at the end of July caused this period in the history of the US Air Force to be known as "Bloody Summer".

The attack on Ploesti alone had cost the 9th USAAF 773 crew members. It was eight months before they had recovered sufficiently to mount a fresh attack on Ploesti.

But just two weeks after Ploesti the 9th USAAF had found a soft under-belly in the German air defences: Austria. There were virtually no anti-aircraft defences there. People had obstinately refused to recognise the potential danger.

The Bf 109 G was being built in series at Wiener Neustädter Flugzeugwerke (WNF). The 9th USAAF which had taken off from Derna encountered virtually no resistance when its 61 B-24s dropped their war load (about 180 tons of bombs and incendiaries) on the factories. The reduction in Bf 109 production was noticeable for about four weeks. This had shown how sensitive to air attack the German arms industry was. Albert Speer, Minister for Munitions and Armaments, recognised this immediately. He spoke to the General der Jagdflieger, Adolf Galland who replied that with three or four times as many fighters the Americans could be beaten. Generalfeldmarschall Milch, Udet's successor as Generalluftzeugmeister, was of the same opinion. Fighter aircraft production would have been sufficient for that, as from January to August 1943 7477 fighter aircraft were delivered. But Hitler needed aircraft on the Eastern Front and in the Mediterranean.

The battle for the Mediterranean theatre in particular absorbed vast numbers of fighter aircraft. Because of Hitler's "Stand fast and fight" policy, orders to retreat always came too late so that aircraft, vehicles and equipment were either destoyed by carpet bombing or simply abandoned through lack of fuel. And that affected the defence of the German Reich.

Although the aircraft factories were achieving record production figures which nobody would have dreamed possible, the number of single-seat fighters in the German Reich only increased from 120 aircraft in March 1943 to 405 serviceable Bf 109s and Fw 190s at the end of August. In addition there were approximately 80 Bf 110s and Me 410s. A proportion of these fighter groups had been formed recently. But now other formations were being withdrawn from the front line: II./JG 27 under Hauptmann Schroer was withdrawn from Southern Italy to Wiesbaden-Erbenheim; II./JG 51 under Hauptmann Rammelt returned to Neubiberg near Munich. Oberstleut-

nant Trautloft had to bring back III.Gr. JG 54, which was involved in the heavy defensive battles in the northern part of the eastern front, to Oldenburg and Nordholz. JG 3 under Oberstleutnant Wilcke was withdrawn from the southern end of the eastern front and, like JG 26 under Major Priller withdrawn from France, it was transferred to the Lower Rhine and Holland. Even the heavy fighters which had been regarded only as night fighters were now used to defend the German Reich. ZG 26 under Major Karl Boehm-Tettelbach was distributed in the area Wundstorf-Quakenbrück-Hildesheim. The hope was that by using the WGr. 21, with which the Bf 110 had been equipped, the heavy fighters would have a chance as they would be able to attack the four-engined bombers from a safe distance without exposing themselves to return fire. At that time the fire power of the B-17 Es and B-17 Fs consisted of eight to ten .5″ machine guns in turrets and side turrets. (It was not for nothing that they were known as "The Flying Fortress".)

August 17 and 18 1943 were to bring two events which had dreadful repercussions for both sides.

Early in the morning of 17 August 1943 Wasserman and Freya equipment detected that there was unusual activity at all the British bases where the 8th USAAF was stationed. In fact at Orfordness and Clacton two groups of B-17s had been briefed to attack the ball-bearing factories at Schweinfurt, and at Lowestoft a further group of B-17s had been briefed to destroy the Messerschmitt factories at Regensburg where the Bf 109 G-6 was built in large-scale series production. This group of 146 bombers was to fly on from Regensburg and across the Mediterranean to Benghazi to complete its mission. The 230 aircraft destined for Schweinfurt were to return to England. Fighter escort could only be provided up to the Belgian frontier. As soon as the direction-finding reports came in from the 1st Fighter Division at Deelen near Arnhem, Generalleutnant von Döring immediately transferred some fighter groups from the North Sea coast to airfields west of the Rhine. Döring's fighter pilot experience went back to 1917 when he had been Richthofen's deputy in Jagdgeschwader 1. He had continued with the Reichswehrfliegertruppe in Lipezk and had become Jagdgruppenkommandeur as early as 1935. He had been successful in becoming Kommodore and then Jafü.

About 10 o'clock the first B-17s, the Regesburg group, were sighted. There was no point in attacking as long as the Republic P-47 Thunderbolts were escorting them. But as soon as the Thunderbolts turned for home the first Fw 190s of II./JG 1 went into the attack. Fw 190 A-5s and Bf 109 G-6s attacked in relays. Even before the formation reached Regensburg at 11.43, fourteen B-17s had already gone down in flames. From this point onwards though there was virtually no fighter defence. There were no fighters in the southeast as the Americans knew very well since attacking Wiener-Neustadt. Nevertheless the B-17s did not escape unscathed and a further ten were shot down by Bf 109 G fighter units stationed in Italy. When the Americans landed in Benghazi and Derna, only 85 of the original 122 aircraft were in a fit state to fly back to Britain. The American combat report referred to the loss of 20 airmen in the attack on Regensburg wheras German sources state the loss of 250 aircrew, though this number probably includes the seriously wounded. The second US bomber group met with an even worse fate.

This formation had been briefed to attack Schweinfurt but bad weather delayed take-off until about midday. 229 B-17 Es and Fs met over the island of Walcheren and then proceeded on a southeasterly course at about 20,000ft. The German fighters which had attacked the Regensburg formation were again ready for action. They did not wait for the escort fighters to turn back but attacked immediately. These aircraft were the Bf 109 G-6s of II./JG 11 and the others quickly followed them. But first of all the Bf 109s engaged the Thunderbolts and Spitfire escort aircraft whilst 5./JG 11, flying Bf 109 G-6/R2s, fired their WGr.21s on to the bombers. There were two direct hits and the bombers exploded. The other B-17s continued roughly in the direction of Mannheim and only then set course for Schweinfurt. On this stretch they were attacked continously by Bf 109 G-6s of II./JG 27, of JG 11, of JG 300 and of JG 50, a freshly assembled formation which was dispersed again in November 1943. Then more Bf 110s of ZG 26 appeared and destroyed more bombers with their WGr.21s, with the result that of the original 229 B-17s only 208 reached Schweinfurt. The return leg of the flight was distressing for the remaining hard-hit B-17s. Of the 376 B-17s that raided Schweinfurt and Regensburg 60 (16%) were shot down. At least twice that number were so badly damaged that they were out of active service for some time at least. Just 300 fighters had achieved this defence success against 376 bombers.

The next night brought a fresh blow for German defences. 600 bombers of the Royal Air Force attacked the German rocket centre at Peenemünde and caused serious damage and loss of life. When the High Command of the Luftwaffe (OKL) received news of this attack, Generaloberst Jeschon-

Bf 109 G-5 during testing of FuG 217 night fighter equipment at the Technisches Versuchskommando at Werneuchen

The same type with
JG 1

Bf 109 G-6/R2 with Wfr. Gr.
21 of Jagdgruppe 50

R2 kit: rocket tube for 21 cm
"Dödel" rocket

Bf 109 G-6/R1 on the eastern front, October 1943 (Geschwader-Adjutant)

Bf 109 G-6 of JG 3

Bf 109 G-6 of III./JG 77 known as "Wanderzirkus Ubben" (Ubben's Travelling Circus)

221

nek, Chief of General Staff of the Luftwaffe, lost his nerve and shot himself. According to Udet he was the second person who felt responsible for the ill-conceived air defences and therefore also for the selection of the Bf 109 as the only standard fighter.

The night and day air raids on German aircraft factories had some short term effect on series production but did not affect it severely. But that was not all. The real restriction on production was the shortage of raw materials. As dozens of new fighter aircraft designs were produced but not built it was necessary to try to make the best of what was available. Production capacity lost through poor planning can be shown from just one example. When the Jumo 222 aircraft engine (a 24-cylinder engine, combined radial and in-line design) was still at the development stage, the Technisches Amt announced the existence of this engine to the aircraft industry and announced that it would be available in the foreseeable future. The Jumo 222 never went into series production but the design departments of all the German aircraft manufacturers erupted in feverish activity. Aircraft were designed which were based on this 2000 PS engine and some of these aircraft were even built and then had to be put to one side because the engines were unavailable. Thousands of working hours were lost as a result. And with the prospect of jet engines the same ritual was repeated. As has already been mentioned, the Generalluftzeugmeister was fundamentally opposed to new developments because he knew that the necessary production capacity simply did not exist. He was more interested in quantity than in quality. Galland, General der Jagdflieger, was exactly the opposite. He would have preferred ten new jet fighters or even

propeller-driven fighters (such as the Dornier Do 335) to one hundred Bf 109s in yet another modified version. It was the fighter pilots flying the old Bf 109 against the totally superior Thunderbolt and Spitfire who had to pay the cost.

Instead of really effective new types of aircraft appearing at the front line there were just new versions of the same old types, types which had been designed before the war such as the Ju 88, He 111, Do 217, Bf 109, Bf 110 and Fw 190. It was not unusual for there to be up to 60 versions of one type.

The scarcity of raw materials already mentioned forced designers to find alternatives. When aluminium became scarce the most usual replacement material was wood. Brass was often replaced by plastic. The Bf 109 G-6/U4 already had a wooden tailplane. That type was to be developed into a new G-7 but the project was abandoned. The successor to the Bf 109 F-5 was the Bf 109 G-8, which was delivered steadily from 1943 onwards to the new short range reconnaissance groups (NAG = NahAufklärungsGruppen) from the old reconnaissance squadrons (H). This version was without the famous bulge as its only weapon was the MK 108 motor-cannon. Rb 12.5/7 or Rb 32/7 automatic cameras were fitted. In addition the G-8 short range reconnaissance aircraft used a "Robot" 35mm camera which was often used by combat pilots to photograph the target immediately after attack. The Robot camera used had a double winder mechanism, ie. it could be used to expose a complete film of 48 shots 24 x 24mm without having to rewind the mechanism after 24 shots. It was fitted in the leading edge of the port wing of the Bf 109 F-5 and G-8; it had a fixed aim and was triggered by a button to the left of the throttle. The observer, who

Bf 109 G-6/U2: Even when defending the Reich the Bf 109 had to rely on 300 litre drop tanks whch reduced its performance considerably

Bf 109 G-6/U2 of II./JG 54

300 litre drop tank with fairing

R4 kit: 300 litre tank under wing

The Italians also flew the Bf 109 G-6. Top and centre: A pilot of 5 Squadriglia, II. Gruppo. Left: Bf 109 G-5 *trop.* of 364. Squadriglia 150. Gruppo of Regia Aeronautica

225

Oberstleutnant Hermann Graf (awarded the Brilliant) of JG 52, after his 200th victory flying the Bf 109 G-6

The installation of the MG 131 above the engine is clearly visible

226

The Bf 109 G-6 was flown too by the Hungarian 5. Staffel of I. Jagdgruppe "Puma"

Centre and bottom: The short range and long range reconnaissance Gruppen both flew the Bf 109 G-6 as a fighter reconnaissance aircraft

was also the pilot of course, was supposed to fly towards the target obliquely and photograph bridges, railway installations, airfields etc. from fairly close to. This facility was not used very often. On the other hand the camera was used widely in dogfights on sorties to confirm possible kills. Some straight fighter aircraft also had this camera mounted in the leading edge of the wing, not only the Bf 109 G but also the Fw 190 A. It had a low power telephoto lens (75mm) for aerial photography. However it would be true to say that fighter pilots and reconnaissance pilots mostly used the camera unofficially for private photographs, which they found easy enough despite the telephoto lens.

Many an action photograph of the Luftwaffe and its aircraft in private hands after the war was taken secretly with this type of camera. This camera was loved by the Allies too. In 1945 hundreds of *Robots* were taken from German Luftwaffe personnel and "liberated" by the Allied soldiers. Although the short-range reconnaissance pilots had a fast aircraft in the Bf 109 G-8, their job was getting more difficult by the day. At the beginning of 1944 they were still able to perform their role successfully on the whole despite all difficulties. On the Eastern front, contact with Soviet fighters in the enemy hinterland and on quieter stretches of the Front were not too frequent. But during 1944 the situation was to change rapidly as we shall see.

The Bf 109 G-8 was flown on virtually all fronts. It was often flown in the Bf 109 G-8/R3 versions with a 300 litre drop tank. The Messerschmitt concern kept working on yet new versions. The Bf 109 G-9 project was abandoned in mid-development. In its place there was intense activity on a new Bf 109 G-10 fighter which did not appear until 1944.

After numerous discussions between Messerschmitt and the Technisches Amt the development of the Me 155 high altitude fighter was transferred to Blohm & Voss in 1943. Dr. Richard Vogt, head of the design team at Blohm & Voss, was a man always bursting with new ideas. He made change after change to the Me 155 design. More and more parts were replaced by redesigned ones so that soon there was little of the project that was still original Messerschmitt. The Me 155 became the Bv 155, the prototype of which was produced at the beginning of 1944.

Meanwhile, what had become of the Me 309 which had already been under development for two years? The Me 309 V1, GE + CU, had made its maiden flight a year previously but was forced to land after seven minutes because of cooling difficulties. The tail itself had to be modified five times. On November 11 1942 Galland was allowed to see the aircraft. It looked very good but . . . it would take a long time for any front line pilot to get to grips with it. It was redesigned GE + CV and then sent for tests without armament fitted. On its maiden flight on 29 November 1942, it was declared a total write-off after damage to the nose. As the Me 309 V1 had also been the V2, the next aircraft was the Me 309 V3, GE + CW, which was tested from March 1943. The Me 309 V4 RH + LH flew for the first time in July 1943. In the meantime, the Me 262 programme had started and the Me 309 was forgotten. The Me 309 was used for testing ejector seat systems and pressurized cabins and Me 309 V4 was used for testing wide track undercarriage and various weapon installations. It was destroyed at Leipheim in an air raid. That was the end of the Me 309 saga.

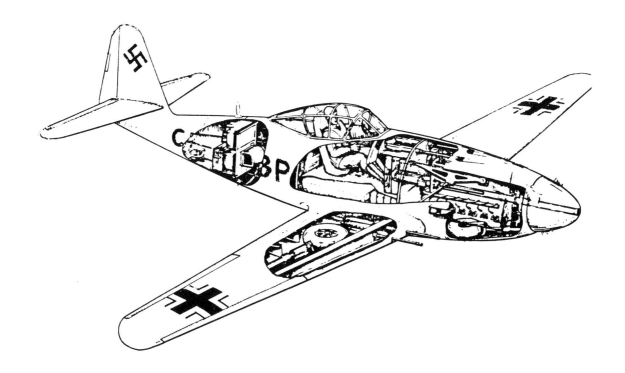

Cut away drawing of Me 309 project

Planned armament arrangements of Me 309

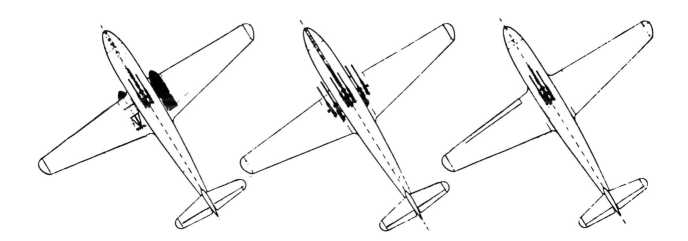

That brought to an end three projects which were partly connected with the Me 209 V5 and partly with the Me 309. Just as with the Bf 109 Z, Messerschmitt had intended to develop a twin fuselage Me 409 from the Me 209 V5. With the great reduction in types resulting from the fighter priority programme, the Me 209 V5 and the Me 409 were shelved in favour of the Ta 152.

The Me 509, which was developed on the basis of the Me 309, had a strange and murky fate. It had a different engine arrangement, similar to the American Bell P-39 Airacobra which had been delivered to the Soviet Union where some examples had fallen into German hands. The pilot was to sit between the propeller and the DB 605 engine over a shaft driving the three bladed propeller. When the Me 309 programme was dropped in 1943/44, the Me 509 programme was also rejected. At about the same time the Yokosuka Navy Arsenal in Japan began to develop an aircraft planned to provide transition to a jet aircraft and this had the same engine arrangement as the Me 509. Interestingly, if you compare the sketch of the Me 509 side view with the few remaining photographs of the Japanese R2Y1 "Keiun" (Cloud of Happiness) you cannot help noticing the unmistakable similarities between the two aircraft. As Messerschmitt had supplied the Bf 109 and the Me 410 to Japan, there is a suspicion that the design for Me 509 also ended up in Japan. The R2Y1 made its maiden flight shortly before the end of the war, too late for a test flying programme to be completed. The Me 609 was a development parallel to the Bf 109 Z, just as the Me 409 had been, but it was to be a combination of 2 Me 309s. The results were disappointing and the Me 609 was also rejected. It is interesting to note, however, that the Americans took up the idea of the twin fuselage aircraft and developed the P-82 from the North American P-51.

The air battle between Regensburg and Schweinfurt had had a sobering effect on the Command of the 8th USAAF. From a report on the operation we read: "The German air defence was exception in its scope, its skilful planning and in the force with which it was carried out." Learning from these losses there were no further air raids for the time being. Italy fell at the beginning of September and the Allies landed on the Italian coast. The Germans reacted quickly and eliminated the Italian forces except for those that had remained loyal to Mussolini.

Milch had pressed on energetically with fighter production, and in July had achieved a peak of 725 Bf 109 Gs and 325 Fw 190 As. But then production fell as the effects of the air raids on Regensburg and Wiener-Neustadt were felt. The production figures of July 1943 were never matched again.

The next time that the 8th USAAF flew over the German Reich was on October 10 1943. They carried out an air raid on Münster, a town without any military target, using bombs and incendiaries dropped from 138 B-17s. Even today no-one seems to know why this town, which was attacked several times again later by the 8th USAAF, was targeted for air raids.

There were smaller raids on Marienburg, Danzig and Münster once again, but then came plans for another air raid on October 14 on Schweinfurt, the ball-bearing town.

If the Schweinfurt works production capacity could be destroyed, it would have a very serious effect on the whole German armaments industry, as over 42% of German ball-bearing production was produced there by VKF (SKF) and FAG. 228 B-17s took off escorted by 103 P-47s. When the formation and its escort reached the Rhine-

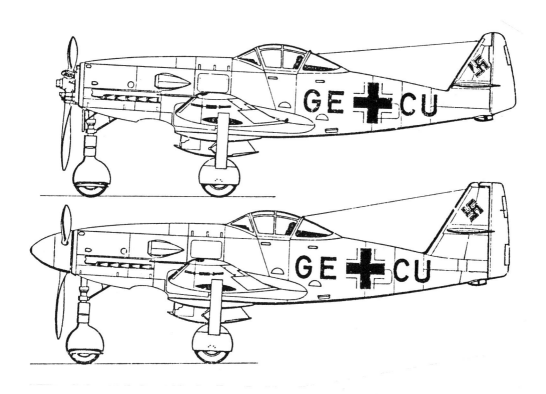

Fin and rudder changes to Me 309 V1. Upper drawing 30.7.1942, lower drawing 9.12.1942

Me 309 V1, GE + CU before its maiden flight

Me 309 V1 after its maiden flight

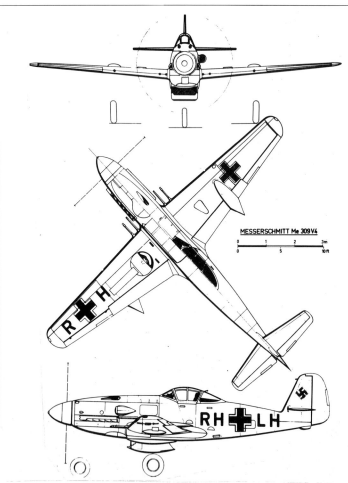

General arrangement drawing of Me 309 V4

MESSERSCHMITT Me 309 V4

0   1   2   3m
0   5   10 ft

land they suffered the first attack by Bf 109 G-6s of JG 11, but they were too weak to break through the American fighter escort. One P-47 was shot down but a number of Bf 109s were so badly damaged that they crash landed. Around Aachen (Aix-la-Chapelle) the P-47s had to turn back or would have run out of fuel. From that moment on the Luftwaffenbefehlshaber Mitte (Luftwaffe Commander in Chief Central), Generaloberst Weise, could deploy his heavy fighters and even night

Opposite page: Comparison of the side view of the Me 509 drawing and photos of the Japanese Yokosuka R2Y1 shows the clear similarity between the two designs

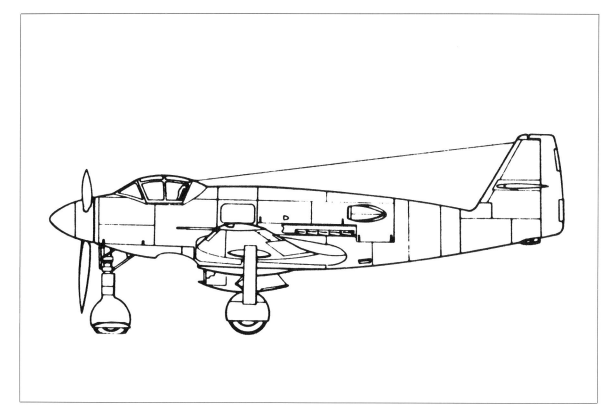

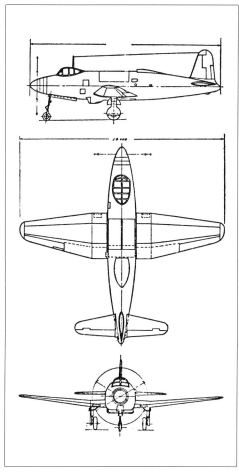

fighters, in such a way that the American bomber crews had not a moment's peace. A further complication for the Americans was the fact that a second bomber formation of the 9th USAAF was supposed to attack the same target from Libya but never took off. The Americans reported that the 228 B-17s were attacked no less than 291 times. The Bf 110s, Bf 109 G-6/R2s and Fw 190 A 4/R6s were particularly effective with their WGr 21s. Out of firing range of the gunners the 21cm rockets were fitted into the formation which split up and the bombers could then be tackled individually.

Reports of losses by the two sides do not tally. The Luftwaffe reported 121 bombers shot down, the Americans admitted 62, but in addition, there were 17 which crashed back in England or were totally written off on landing. A further 121 B-17s were so badly damaged that about a third of them had to be scrapped. The Americans claimed to have shot down 186 German fighters and heavy fighters. The OKL log entry stated that 360 fighters, heavy fighters and night fighters were deployed and that 38 were shot down and 51 seriously damaged. These latter figures are probably correct. The shooting down of the B-17s meant the loss of over 1000 aircrew as the B-17 had a complement of 10. Aircrew losses on the German side were significantly less. The Americans, however, had no problem in replacing lost airmen but for the Germans it was much more difficult. Schweinfurt was one of the last great defence successes for German fighters. But those who could read the situation knew that soon the Americans would be returning with long range fighters to protect their bombers from attack by German fighters and what would happen then? Galland ordered the fastest and best fighters to protect German airspace. Only if the number of high performance fighters roughly matched the present superior numbers of the enemy would it be possible to prevent air raids on the German Reich and the strength of the German armaments industry being sapped. His ideas fell on deaf ears. Hitler rejected them as nonsense and Göring spoke of the "fantasies of a defeatist weakling". After all, with the Bf 109 and the Fw 190 at hand what could go wrong? The only immediate outcome was that the Luftwaffe was reorganised. General Kammhuber, who had set up the night fighter arrangements, resigned and went to Norway as Head of Luftflotte 5. The previous Head of Luftflotte 5, Generaloberst Stumpf, replaced Lufftwaffenbefehlshaber Central, Generaloberst Weise, who became Head of a newly created "Luftflotte Reich". The XII. Fliegerkorps was renamed the I. Jagdkorps and consisted of the Fighter Divisions 1, 2, 3 and 7. Jagddivisionen 4 and 5 were combined to create a II. Jagdkorps. Two new posts were Inspekteur of Day Fighters and Inspekteur of Night Fighters. Head of the night fighters was Oberst Hermann, but he was soon replaced by one of the oldest and most experienced night fighter pilots, Oberstleutnant Streib. Daytime fighters were divided into three areas: "Day Fighters East" under Oberstleutnant Trautloft, "Day Fighters West and South" under Oberstleutnant Lützow. This organisation known as "Reichsverteidigung" (Defence of the Reich) which had been Galland's creation, remained through to the end of the war in 1945. There was a breakdown in the relationship between Göring and Galland, and Galland offered to resign and serve on the front line. Göring agreed.

In the meantime, the Americans were making further preparations for the total aerial bombardment of Germany. On October 22 1943 they started in Italy to assemble the 15th USAAF whose task was to attack the south eastern area, including Southern Germany and Austria.

There was another heavy air raid on Kassel on the night of 22/23 October. The enemy aircraft could only be attacked as they were turning to go home when JG 300 with its Bf 109 G-6s was able to shoot down a number of bombers silhouetted against the enormous fires below.

For the time being the 8th USAAF held back until November 3rd when a formation of about 400 B-17 bombers carried out an air raid on Wilhelmshaven. The sodden surface of deployment of Jagdgeschwader 1 and 11. Using their H2S radar equipment, the Americans were now able to bomb without the ground being visible. They suffered virtually no losses, especially as Republic P-47s with extended range drop tanks were now able to defend the bombers.

From the middle of November to the beginning of December, 1943, there were repeated heavy air raids on Berlin. Night fighters, including JG 300 and 301, with Bf 109 G-6s, succeeded in shooting down 123 British bombers. But that could not bring back the 2,700 dead or turn back the clock on the damage.

The 8th USAAF carried out an air raid on Bremen again on 26 November. JG 1 and JG 11 were successful in shooting down some of the bombers. But on 13 December 1,462 American B-17s, B-24s, B-26s (Martin Marauders) and B-25s appeared in the skies over Kiel, Bremen, Hamburg and Schiphol airport and carried out the biggest daylight raid yet. The handful of Bf 109 and Fw 190 German fighters were completely ineffective against these numbers. The most they could do was to produce a minor irritation. The men responsible for the defence of the Reich became increasingly aware of the fact that the Reich could not be defended any longer with the means at their disposal. This was underlined on 15 December 1943 when American bombers, flying from North Africa, raided Innsbruck in the Austrian Tyrol, an area where there were virtually no air defences. Allied preparations for the invasion of France began on December 24 1943 with the appointment of General Eisenhower as Commander-in-Chief of the operation.

Flying this Me 109 G-6, RU + OZ, a German pilot landed at Samedan, Switzerland, on March 29 1944

A German pilot landed this Bf 109 G-6 at an American airfield near Santa Maria, Italy, on July 25 1944

This captured aircraft (FE 496) was extremely carefully restored in the American National Air and Space Museum in Washington and prepared in the markings of the Stab JG 27 and given Works no. 160163. Before (above) and after restoration

One of the Bf 109 F-4s of I./JG 54
on the eastern front

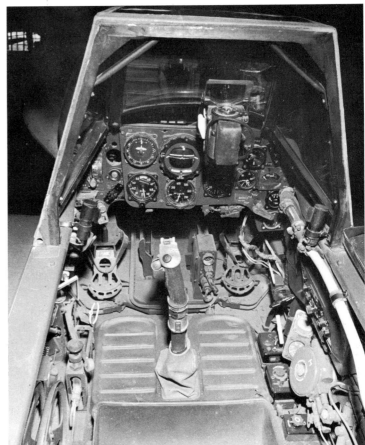

The cockpit – carefully
reconstructed using components
from crashed aircraft

10. Desperate Struggle on all Fronts From the Bf 109 G-10 to the Bf 109 K

1944 saw the creation of the "United States Strategic Air Forces in Europe (USSTAF)". From now on German armament capacity was to be systematically destroyed.

USSTAF's first operation was to raid the Junkers factories in Halberstadt and Magdeburg, AGO in Oschersleben and MIAG in Brunswick with 663 B-17s and B-24s escorted by P-47s with drop tanks and the first North American P-51 B "Mustang" long range fighters. Why these targets? Tailplanes for the Ju 88/188 were built in Halberstadt, Junkers aircraft engines in Magdeburg, the Fw 190 in Oschersleben and the Do 217 in Brunswick. The German fighter divisions Jagd-Divisionen 1, 2 and 3 managed to oppose the Americans with 239 Bf 109 G-6s and Fw 190 As. 239 aircraft but only 207 of them managed to break through the American escort fighter protection and get at the bombers. Some of the bombers were the new B-17G series which had the nose turret with two .5" machine guns. If a German fighter attacked head-on it was now flying into the sights of machine guns. The German fighter pilots did all they could and shot down 59 four-engine bombers and 5 escort fighters but 40 Bf 109s and Fw 190s were lost in this battle.

The major Soviet attack on the Leningrad front started three days later and led to a breakthrough of the German lines. In Italy Allied attacks against the Gustav line began. In Britain a draft plan for the division of Germany along the line Lübeck-Helmstedt-Eisenach-Hof was discussed (15.1.44). Hitler's only response was retaliation raids of IX. Fliegerkorps (whch had about 450 aircraft) on London and other towns in the south east of England. But on 29 January 806 bombers of the USAAF raided Frankfurt and Ludwigshafen. The only defence success was the shooting down of 12 B-17s by Jagdgeschwader 3.

Raids on German aircraft factories continued. 20 February 1944 saw a raid by 971 US bombers on Brunswick, Leipzig, Oschersleben, Tutow and the Focke-Wulf factories at Posten.

German fighters were still desperately trying to break through the fighter escort. They didn't have much chance against the Mustang. They shot down 13 Mustangs but managed to down only 7 bombers out of 971. Flak was more successful. 85 B-17s returned to base with sufficient flak damage to be unserviceable in the immediate future.

The strain under which the Luftwaffe was operating can be seen from the loss reports of 31 January 1944: in January 1944 1115 German fighter aircraft were shot down.

German production figures would have remained much lower if it had not been for the initiative of Minister of Munitions and

Armanents Speer and Secretary of State Milch who had founded the "Jägerstab" headed by the Hauptamtsleiter of the NSDAP, Karl Saur. It is difficult to describe in full what this organisation achieved in rapid reconstruction of bomb-damaged factories and in the systematic decentralisation of the German aircraft industry. There was no bureaucracy, no paperwork, but everything went quickly and smoothly. The Jägerstab was also responsible for the "Jägernotpro-gramm" (fighter priority programme). Apart from reconnaissance aircraft which were desperately needed, production was restric-ted to fighters, fighter bombers, night fighters and ground attack aircraft. Bomber production was ruthlessly cut back.

But it was all too late. Above all it was Hitler's obstinacy in insisting at all costs on a "blitz bomber" which had delayed pro-duction of the superior Me 262 jet fighter by months.

And now the Americans put on their so-called "Big Week". Between 20 and 25 February a total of 3800 four-engined bombers of the 8th and 15th USAAF hammered German aircraft factories. They lost 226 bombers and 28 Mustangs to German fighters and flak. But it was not just the Americans who were losing air crew — the German fighter formations were too. The Americans could cope with these losses, but the Germans were past doing so.

The German fighters were increasingly on the defensive. The fighters were not alone in being under pressure. Increasingly the short-range reconnaissance groups equip-ped with Bf 109 G-8s found that their task was hopeless. Being numerically inferior, German reconnaissance pilots had little chance from 1944 onwards. This was true of the West and South just as much as the East. A few old Henschel Hs 126s were still lurking in the Balkans. On the Eastern Front the Fw 189 which had been deployed in large numbers in 1943 increasingly had to be replaced by the Bf 109 G-8 except where the Fw 189 was given fighter protection in the form of a pair of Bf 109s or Fw 190s. Even the Bf 109 G-8 had little chance when engag-ing Soviet fighter aircraft. In spite of these factors experienced airmen with a few tricks up their sleeve were still able to complete missions. Whereas in 1943 they had been able to shoot down Russian fighters fairly frequently, it only happened rarely in 1944. But if a Bf 109 G-8/R3 penetrated deep into the Russian hinterland it rarely met Soviet fighters. Up to the middle of 1944 they were able to escape from Soviet fighter formations. The Russian fighter aircraft could initially climb more rapidly than the Bf 109 but if the climb continued above 20,000ft the Soviet fighters gave up. This was true of dog fights between German and Soviet fighter aircraft as well. On one occasion for example a pair of Bf 109 G-8s encountered eight Soviet fighters flying at about 12,500ft. The German fighters at-tacked the Russian formation in the middle from below which then immediately split up and made no effort to pursue the two Bf 109s. In the Summer of 1944 the new Soviet Yakolev Yak 3 appeared. This was a parallel development to the Yak 9, but designed specially for low level work. That was the end of the Fw 189 — it couldn't even be used with fighter escort from now on. Of course every reconnaissance fighter pro-duced was one less fighter aircraft pro-duced. But it was not just the short range reconnaissance aircraft that were meeting problems. Although successful at first, the much-vaunted "Wilde Sau" policy turned out in 1944 to have been a mistake. In the Autumn of 1943 Göring had ordered the

Bf 109 G-6/R5 with Mk 108 under the wings

Ammunition for a Bf 109/U4/R5 MK 108

JG 53 airfield in Italy ablaze after an Allied air
raid

The Bf 109 G-6/R6 armed with 2 MG 131s and 3 MG 151/20s was to become the most common type during the closing months of the war

Bf 109 G-6/U 2/R6 over Italy (above) and Bf 109 G-6/U 2/R6 on active service in Italy (below)

creation of two more single-seat night fighter groups JG 301 and JG 302; JG 301 to be allocated to Bavaria and JG 302 to the Brandenburg region, ie. defending the capital, Berlin. The standard Bf 109 G-6 had proved inadequately armed for effective use against four-engined day and night bomber formations. The fighter groups defending the German Reich were increasingly equipped with the series produced Bf 109 G-6/R6. In addition to the normal two MG 131s over the engine, an MG 108 motor cannon or MG 151/20, it had two MG 151/20s in pods under the wings. As the four-engined bombers generally flew at about 20,000ft there was no need for a pressurized cabin. For altitudes in excess of this, there was an oxygen system for the pilot.

At Göring's request Oberstleutnant Hermann, the father of the "Wilde Sau" policy, was given his own responsibility, the 30th Jagd-Division (Fighter Division). Göring's order was clear: "Oberstleutnant Hermann as the creator of this new tactic should also be in a position to lead the operation. He will be directly responsible to the Luftwaffe Commander (Central Germany) with a post created for him (30th Jagd-Division). JG 300, 301, 302 and the Beleuchtergruppe (Pathfinder Group) III.KG 3 are directly under the control of Oberstleutnant Hermann in every respect."

As early as the Winter of 1943/44 it was obvious that single-seat fighters were very sensitive to visibility problems in bad weather and at night. Hermann had set incredibly tough take-off criteria for the single-seat night fighters which resulted in a number of accidents, many of them fatal. After completing their sortie many Bf 109 G-6/R6s crashed because for one reason or another they couldn't find an airfield in time. Running out of fuel (again

the result of the Bf 109's inadequate range) was often the cause but interference and overcrowding on airfield homing frequencies also contributed. A further problem was that British Mosquitoes forced the airfields to leave their landing lights extinguished except for very short periods. After Generaloberst Stumpf had become Chef der Reichsverteidigung, 30. Jagd-Division was placed under I. Jagdkorps led by Generalleutnant "Beppo" Schmidt. III./KG 3 was renamed I.(Bel.)KG 7. This group, like the other pathfinder groups, had the task of directing night fighters to the enemy bombers. Parts of I./JG 300 were transferred to II./NJG 1 to fight the Mosquitoes which were becoming an increasing problem. Single engine night fighters were less and less successful. In 1944 the twin-engined night fighters achieved 230 kills whereas the single-engined fighters only managed about 50. On 31 August 1944 Oberstleutnant Hermann reported that in his command area about 75-80 kills had been achieved by 55 pilots since 12 July.

When the invasion began the Bf 109 G-6/R6 of I./JG 301 had been ordered to Chateaudun, Coulommiers and Epinoy in France. The group was reinforced by men of the 9./ZG 1 and then used to protect the V-1 (Fi 103) launching ramps with some success. Single engine night fighter flying had virtually stopped by now. JG 300, 301 and 302 were now flying almost exclusively daytime sorties. The individual wings of this group were now only used separately and put at the disposal of other units. They were gradually disbanded between the Summer of 1944 and the end of the war. In May 1945 the last wing of this fighter group, III./JG 300, ceased to exist. In Spring 1944 the delivery of the Bf 109 G-10 had begun. The G-10 was largely similar to the G-6 but enjoyed the following improvements: the Daimler-Benz DB 605-A-1 was replaced by versions AM, AS, D-1, DB or DC. Armament and equipment was that of the G-6, but the undercarriage had been strengthened to cope with the higher loads resulting from modifications and additions. Many of these aircraft were fitted with dust filters on the supercharger inlet. The most noticeable change from the G-6 was the so-called "Galland-Haube" (Galland canopy). Previously the canopy had been a two-piece unit whereas this one-piece canopy not only gave the pilot better visibility but was also quicker to jettison in an emergency. The G-10 was flown as a fighter or fighter bomber as required. It was clear that there was now an urgent need to provide fighter pilots with more intensive training as the training hours a pilot received had reduced progressively. For this purpose a G-5, works number 18391, CJ+MG, was converted to Bf 109 V52 for experimental work. A second seat and dual controls were added. The MG 131 and the motor cannon were removed to compensate for the increased weight. Generally there were just two MG 17s and only a few aircraft had the MK 108 motor cannon installed. Altogether eighty Bf 109 G-1s and G-5s were converted to G-12s which were delivered to various relief wings and squadrons. Whereas every Jagdgeschwader had its relief Gruppe or Staffel (wing or squadron) up to 1943, from 1944 onwards these were independent formations which generally carried the JG numbers 100 to 110.

Things didn't always go right for the Americans either, as was seen with the planned daylight raid by the 8th USAAF on 3 March 1944. The weather was so bad that none of the bombers could take off and only a few Mustangs reached the outer limits of Berlin. When the Americans renewed the attack three days later in bright sunshine they found stiff resistance from fighters and flak. 627 B-17s and B-24s dropped 1600 bombs and incendiaries on the capital of the Reich and increased the flattened area of rubble in the city. The whole of 1. Jagd-Korps attacked the American formation time and time again. Some squadrons had the opportunity to attack the enemy twice. The tactics had been changed: whilst some of the squadrons kept the Mustangs busy, others, mainly Fw 190s, got through to the bombers with the result that 68 bombers, mainly B-24s, and 11 Mustangs, were shot down. The Americans noticed the losses for on the next day only 540 B-17s with fighter escort returned to Berlin. The German fighters had losses too which could not be made good immediately. This time 38 B-17s and 16 Mustangs were shot down. A day later 330 B-17s returned to Berlin but only six were brought down by flak. The fighters had not a single success to report.

The retreat from the Eastern Front gradually became a serious business. The raids by the 8th USAAF on the German aircraft industry continued incessantly. The air raids on the centre of the German ball-bearing industry at Schweinfurt were repeated, but because of decentralisation of production they did not succeed in taking out this key industry. In May 1944 the 15th USAAF concentrated its attacks on German fuel installations in the South East. The main target was of course the oil wells at Ploesti in Rumania. But now refineries in Austria, Hungary and Yugoslavia were also attacked. In addition the Royal Air Force began to drop mines in the Danube by night as this was an important shipping route on which a major proportion of the Rumanian oil was transported to Germany. It was only now that serious steps were taken to deal

Bf 109 G-10/U2. This photo gives a good impression of the Galland cockpit cover (J Gr 50)

Works drawing of Bf 109 G-10

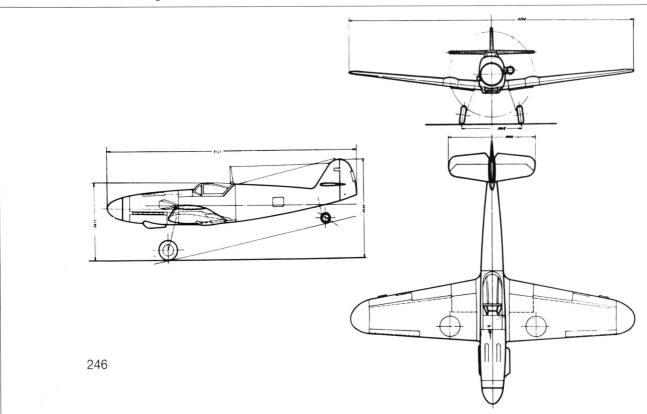

Bf 109 G-6/R2 *trop.* of
9./JG 3

Bf 109 G-6/R6 of
JG 50

Bf 109 G-6 *trop.*,
Works no. 16416

247

with this threat. Certainly the "Kommando" Jafü Ostmark was already in existence and there had been two fighter wings and a heavy fighter wing in it. But on 15 June 1944, the 8. Jagd-Division was formed under Oberst Handrick, based at Vienna-Kobenzl. Under him were II./JG 27, I./JG 302, II./ZG 1, III./NJG 6 and II./JG 10 and also fighter training school JG 108 as a reserve formation.

Apart from the heavy fighters, all the formations flew Bf 109 G-6s and some of them G-6/R6 and the operational squadrons of JG 108 flew Bf 109 G-5s. But it was not only in the south eastern area that the oil industry was under attack but also in Central Germany, even in Bohemia & Moravia, bombs fell on refineries and oil installations and installations producing synthetic fuel. The loss in production was enormous: it was generally 50% but in individual cases such as Tröglitz it was even total.

On 21 May the Americans began the systematic destruction of all transport routes in France, Belgium and Holland. Two days later the Allies launched an offensive in Italy. Two days later the Allies launched an offensive in Italy. Germany retreated here too. The army divisions were virtually defenceless against the Allied air attacks. There were simply not enough fighters.

On 4 June the Allies took Rome. Two days later "Operation Overlord" began with the Allies landing in Normandy.

Just how complete Allied air superiority was is shown from the following figures: on 6 June 1944 the Allied Air Forces flew 145,674 missions. The German Luftflotte 3 led by Generalfeldmarschall Sperrle flew 260 missions during the day and 59 at night.

The destruction of German aircraft factories produced an enforced simplification of the Bf 109 design. The result was the Bf 109 G-14. The airframe was generally similar to the G-10 but had a simplified undercarriage fairing and the tailwheel was non-retractable. Instead of the MK 108, which had not always proved reliable, the MG 151/120 was installed. The fighter-bomber version G-14/R1 was more heavily armoured. Most of these aircraft had the water methanol MW50 emergency power boost system. Only a few aircraft had wooden tailplanes. The Bf 109 G-14s used in defence of the German Reich flew with the R6 modification – two MG 151/120s in pods under the wings. G-10s and G-14s sometimes had the U4 modification of two additional MK 108s in a pod under the fuselage. This pod was later replaced by a fixed fuel tank known as the "Irmer-Behälter".

In the meantime the Americans continued bombing raids on the German petroleum manufacturing and refining installations. On 20 June 1944 alone, 1500 bombers with an escort of 1000 P-51 Mustangs and P-38 Lightnings, raided fuel refineries in north west and central Germany. The Fighter Divisions of Luftflotte Reich, which were suffering extreme attrition, fought bitterly against the air superiority which was growing daily. Even the old Bf 110 G heavy fighters were occasionally successful.

In the attack on Pölitz near Stettin Bf 110 Gs of ZG 76 under Major Kowalewski shot down 15 B-17 Fs with the WGr 21. Two Bf 110s were lost. The German fighter pilots showed their teeth again: 50 B 17s and five Mustangs were shot down for the loss of 28 Bf 109s and Fw 190s. 468 B-17s and B-24s returned to base so badly damaged that they were unserviceable. Despite that, on the next day approximately 2500 American bombers and fighters attacked railway installations and aircraft and engine fac-

Bf 109 G-6/R6 before
allocation

Bf 109 G-6/R6 of III.
(Sturm)/JG 3

Bf 109 G-6/R6/R3 of
the Kommandeur of
I./JG 27

Unteroffizier Hans Seyringer of 2./JG 27 with his Bf 109 G-6/U4

A Bf 109 G-6, shot down at Tilly-sur-Seulles being investigated by British soldiers, June 1944

Bf 109 G-6/R6 during the battle for Stalingrad at Pitomnik

Bf 109 G-6/R6 of I./JG 300, October 1943 (Defence of the Reich)

Two Bf 109 G-6/R3/R6 *trop.* of I./JG 27

Bf 109 G-6/R6 of III./JG 53 in Italy

Bf 109 G-8 after the collapse in 1945, Bardufoss, Norway

A Bf 109 G-8/R5 of 1.(H) 32 at Bodö/Norway seen here with Norwegian soldiers, May 1945

Bf 109 G-10 at the end of the war, 1945

Bf 109 G-10/R3 on the approach

Bf 109 G-10 at Salzburg at the end of the war

Maintenance work on a carefully camouflaged Bf 109 G-10/R3

Bf 109 G-10/U2 taxiing to the runway

A pilot of 15.(Croatia)/JG 52 defected to the Americans at Falconara in Italy flying this Bf 109 G-10/R3

Bf 109 G-10 *trop.* of the Finnish H. Le. Lv.33

Bf 109 G-10/R1 of III./JG 3 ready for a fighter bomber sortie

Bf 109 G-10 with "Irmer-Behälter"

tories in the Berlin area. 44 B-17s and B-24s were shot down by fighter pilots of 1. Jagd-korps. But then the Americans suffered a severe setback: 114 B-17s and 70 Mustangs separated from the formation and flew on towards Russia. Most of the bombers landed in Poltava and the fighters in Pirjatin. They were unaware that a He 177 had followed them and noticed where they had landed. The He 177 reported back and Generalleutnant Meister, head of the IV. Fliegerkorps, got together 200 He 111s and Ju 88s of KG 3, 4, 53 and 55 and attacked the airfields by night. The total supply of bombs and fuel which the Americans had stored there and 47 B-17s were totally destroyed and the remaining aircraft damaged. After that the Americans gave up trying to carry out 'pendulum raids'.

Success of that sort was rare as the situation in the east was becoming more desperate for fighter pilots and reconnaissance pilots. The new Yak 3 and Yak 9, La 5 FN and La 7, totally outclassed the German Bf 109 G-6s and Fw 190 A-6s. It was only in armament that the German fighters were superior. Russian fighter defence against German reconnaissance aircraft strengthened continuously from the Summer of 1944. As soon as German reconnaissance aircraft crossed the Soviet lines they were shot at by well-aimed flak. The smoke from the exploding flak drew the attention of Russian fighter pilots to the German Bf 109 G-8s. And it was not unusual for 10 to 15 La 5s or Yak 3s to go into the attack. In the latter half of 1944 German reconnaissance fighters suffered an alarming increase in damage and write-offs. In the battles on the invasion front the Luftwaffe tried out a new weapon experimentally against the Allied landing fleet, a weapon which involved the Bf 109 G-6: the

"Beethoven" device, generally referred to as "Mistel" (mistletoe). The Beethoven device consisted of a Bf 109 mounted on the back of a Ju 88 which was piloted to its target by the fighter pilot. In the nose of the Ju 88 was a hollow charge weighing 3.7 tons with a fuse. The fighter pilot flying the composite aircraft dived steeply at the target, released the Ju 88 at a safe height and left it to home in on the target on auto-pilot. The fighter pilot attempted to leave the scene as quickly as possible.

This project went back to experiments by the Deutsche Forschungsanstalt für Segelflug "Ernst Udet" (German Gliding Research Institute) led by Fritz Stamer, the grand old man of gliding. The tests centred around a type of aero-tow. On page 8 of the study produced by Stamer he mentions the 'Mistelschlepp' (mistletoe aero-tow) as the seventh method. In it he says that rigid towing such as used for the DFS 230 and Go 242 was not possible for modern fighter aircraft although their engine power would be sufficient. And then Stamer went on: "To find a solution to this problem and to use the fighter aircraft which are available in large numbers for towing, which do have major tactical advantages over other aircraft after release in terms of air speed and fire power, the Mistel system was developed by the flight testing institute of the DFS." The test version consisted of a DFS 230 troop carrying glider with a Klemm Kl 35 mounted on top of it. For the second test a Focke-Wulf Fw 56 developing barely 100 PS more was used to power it. Tests showed that it could take off carrying the empty troop carrier. But the third test version with a Bf 109 E mounted above the DFS 230 was convincing. The Bf 109 engine was sufficient to take off with the DFS 230.

Composite developement was then transferred from the DFS to Junkers. The main problem was the question of control connections but a suitable breakable linkage between the control system of the lead Bf 109 and the lower aircraft was soon developed. This opened up the way to the complete "Beethoven-Gerät" composite. In early tests combinations of Ju 88A-4 as the lower aircraft and the Bf 109 G-6 as the lead aircraft were tried and at this stage there was still a co-pilot in the Ju 88. The Ju 88A-4 was converted in Merseburg and the explosives were installed in Nordhausen. These piggy-back aircraft (the Luftwaffe referred to them as "Huckepack-Flugzeuge") were first used during the invasion. An attack on the British fleet in Scapa Flow using the Beethoven-Gerät had been planned. As this was very successful (though the surprise factor should not be forgotten), the so-called "Mistel" programme was commenced. The author, who was involved in this programme at the Junkers-Werft Leipzig, has written about it in his book on the Ju 88 and its successors. Further details and experiences can be read in Stahl: *Geheim-Geschwader KG 200*. Both books are published by Motorbuch Verlag Stuttgart. As the lead aircraft was later usually an Fw 190 A-6 or A-8 the further development of this system has little to do with the Bf 109.

The battle against the American four-engined bombers became increasingly difficult. After individual pilots had rammed the Flying Fortresses on their own initiative, so-called "Sturmgruppen" (Storm Groups) were created within the fighter groups. General Fw 190s were used for this purpose and also Me 109 G-6/R6/R3s with additional armour. When the 8th USAAF attacked Leipzig and Oschersleben on 7 July 1944 with large numbers of bombers the Sturmjäger of IV./JG 3 were particularly success-

ful over Oschersleben. A large number of the 58 B-24s shot down on that day were the work of the Me 109s of this group. Other German fighters shot down a further 24 escort fighters.

In August 1944 Jagdkommandos for air defence of fixed installations and anti-Mosquito work were formed from parts of 1./NJGr. 10 and 6. and 10.JG 300. At the end of August the remains of 6./JG 300 became 1./NJG 11 and parts of 1./NJGr. 10 became 2./NJG 11. All these squadrons were equipped with Fw 190 A-8s, Bf 109 G-6/R6s and Bf 109G-14s. The Bf 109 G-6, G-10 and G-14 were now only playing a minor role in night fighter work, the reason being that it was impossible to equip the Bf 109 G with antlerhorn aerials because of the leading edge slats. It was only possible to fit FuG Neptune J3 rod aerials. NJG 11 flew pursuit fighters and area night fighters through till January 1945 and after that the aircraft were all converted to fighter bombers with field modification kit R1, ETC 500 or 503 bomb carriers and only used as night ground attack aircraft. "Schräge Musik" (diagonal music), the fixed weapon that fired diagonally upwards, was often used in twin-engined night fighters but so far as is known the only example of it installed in a single-seat fighter was the Bf 109 G-14 of Major Müller of NJG 11.

The short range reconnaissance aircraft in the East and in the West fared no better. From early in the morning enemy fighters patrolled over the airfields of the short range reconnaissance squadrons and as soon as a Bf 109 G-8 tried to take off it was attacked. In the closing weeks of the war the short range reconnaissance pilots felt safer in the air than at their own air bases. They were rarely in a position to fulfil their role satisfactorily as they were involved in

Bf 109 G-10 being overhauled

Bf 109 G-10 of I./JG 53 after this airfield in Italy had been taken by the Americans

DFS experiment,
"Mistel-Schlepp"
(Mistletoe composite)
Bf 109 E, together
with DFS 230

First test version of
Mistel Aerotow
Ju 88 C with Bf 109 G-6

Service version
Mistel 1: Ju 88
A-4/Bf 109 F-4

259

Bf 109 V 52, Works no. 18319, CJ+MG, went to JG 104 Jagdschule (fighter training school) on completion of tests

Bf 109 G-12 of a Jagdschule somewhere in the Reich

**Bf 109 G-12 of JG 101
Jagdschule
Pau-Nord (France)**

**More photographs of
JG 101 which show
the construction of
the G-12 version of
the Bf 109 clearly**

dogfights immediately after take-off. Relentlessly the Soviet armies in the East and the other Allies to the West and to the South pressed on. On the Eastern Front the whole of the German 4th Army had been annihilated south of Minsk by 8 July 1944. In the course of two weeks 28 divisions with approximately 350,000 men were eliminated from battle. Even the pilots didn't always succeed in escaping.

In the desperate attempt to find some means of defence against the flow of Allied bombers, the oddest of ideas came up, although everyone knew that it was much too late to develop new weapons. One of these ''Wunderwaffen'' (miracle weapons) in which the Bf 109 G was to have played a role was the ''Fliegende Panzerfaust'' (flying mailed fist). This mini-aircraft with reclining pilot and with a make-do arrangement of six solid fuel rockets to power it was to have been carried to altitude by the Bf 109 G and released at the appropriate moment. The pilot lay protected behind an armoured bulkhead. It was claimed that aircraft was difficult to hit because of its diminutive dimensions. After releasing from the 109 the pilot was supposed to home in on the enemy aircraft using his solid fuel rockets and then fire both his offensive rockets. After that he was to bale out together with reclining seat pan as the whole seat pan complete with headrest dropped out of the bottom of the aircraft. Only after reaching a reasonable speed was the seat pan to be jettisoned. This aircraft never saw operational service.

The 15th USAAF based in Italy concentrated its attacks on the Rumanian oil areas and the oil refineries in Austria. Hungarian fighter formations, which were also equipped with the Bf 109 G-6/R6, supported the German fighter formations up to 12 October 1944.

On 19 July 1944 storms wrought havoc: the Allied convoys were torn apart and the artificial harbour in the ''Omaha'' section was destroyed, producing a crisis situation. On the German side there was little appreciation of these problems because of preoccupations there too. Generalfeldmarschall Rommel was seriously wounded on 17 July in his transport at St. Foy de Montgomery by a Spitfire of 602 squadron of the Royal Air Force doing a low level attack. On the same day the Americans on the invasion front dropped the first napalm bombs. In Italy the Allies progressed and on 19 July Leghorn was taken. Then there was the unsuccessful attempt on Hitler's life on 20 July.

In the meantime at Messerschmitt they were working on a new version of the Bf 109, the Bf 109 K. The pre-production prototypes of this new version were converted from normal G-6s at the beginning of August 1944. These aircraft had the DB 605D, which produced 1800 PS when using MW 50 power boost for take-off and emergency power, which was fitted as standard. The DB 605DM differed from the normal DB 605D only in that it had an injection ring jet for injecting the water/methanol mixture into the super charger intake. In addition there were special spark plugs and a different fuel-injection pump. This motor was tuned for the higher supercharger pressure needed for the emergency power boost. Increasing supercharging pressure at the same time as using MW 50 injection produced increased level air speed and an improved rate of climb. But the MW 50 injection system could only be used up to an altitude of about 28,000 ft. Above that it was useless. Emergency power could be used for ten minutes duration – twice. There had to be a break of at least five minutes between the

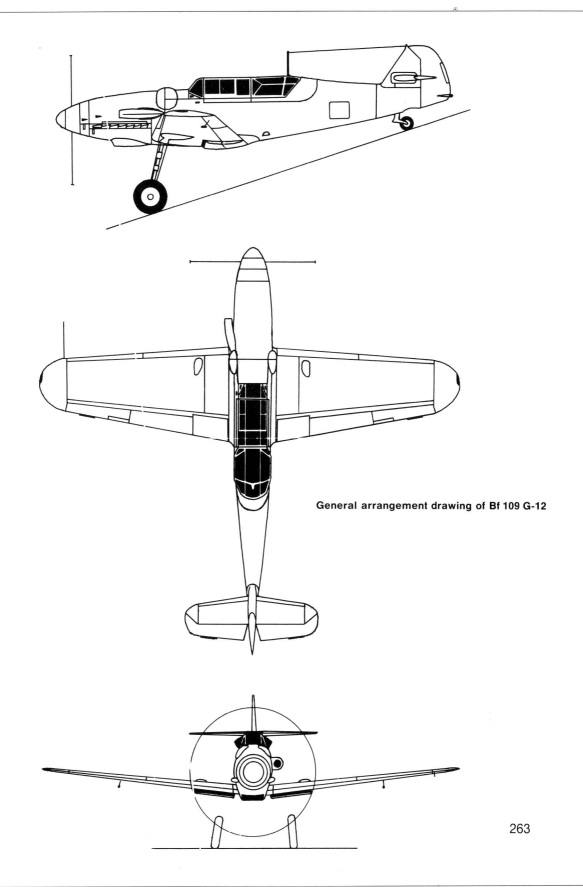

General arrangement drawing of Bf 109 G-12

263

two sessions, during which the aircraft was flown under normal power . . .

Whilst the K-0 tests were continuing, the G-14 was developed into the G-16 fighter bomber which was basically equivalent to the G-14/R1 but more heavily armed. It was powered by the DB 605 D. It was armed with two MG 131s over the engine, an MG 151/20 motor cannon and two MG 151/20s in pods under the wings. In addition there was an ETC 250 stores carrier under the fuselage to take an SC 250 bomb. Only a few examples of the G-16 were built and even fewer saw operational service.

The test-flying on the K-0 resulted in a few modifications. The K-2 series version had the same armament as K-0 and a larger wooden tail which increased the length of the K-2 to 8.94m.

The K2 was powered by both the DB 605-ASCM and also the DB 605DCM. Whilst the K version was, in many respects, the same as the G series the field modification kits were very different:

R1 = ETC 500 or ETC 503 under the fuse-
     lage to provide for bombs up to 500 kg
R2 = ETC 504/VIIId for four SC 50 bombs
     (rarely fitted)
R3 = ETC 503 for 300 litre drop tank
R4 = 2 MG 151/20s in pods under the wings
     (equivalent to the R 6 in the previous
     series)
R5 = 2 MK 108s in pods under the wings
R6 = Installation of BSK 16 robot camera in
     the leading edge of the port wing.

The Bf 109 K-2 was not operational before the winter of 1944/45 because of continued air raids on the aircraft factories.

This also applies to the K-4 series which was designed in 1944. It was similar to the K-2 but had a pressurized cabin which was tried out on some of the K-0 series. There was a choice of engines: DB 605ASC, D-1, DB or DC. Basic armament was originally two MG 131 and a MK 108 motor cannon but later this was replaced by the MK 103. All the field modification kits apart from R 2 were used with the 21cm mortars. The K-4 was able to attack enemy formations flying at very high altitude as it had a ceiling of 41,000 ft. and a maximum speed of 478 mph, though this was when aerodynamically clean – i.e. without field modification kit additions.

In the meantime, the German armies were being forced back further and further. At the end July/beginning August Soviet forces were already in the Baltic and in Poland. In Italy the German troops had been pushed back to south of Florence. The oilfields of Drogobytsch in Galicia had been lost. In the middle of August the Allies landed on the French mediterranean coast between Toulon and Cannes. A German 5th Panzer army offensive against the Americans, who had broken through near Avranches, was unsuccessful despite the support of 300 Bf 109 Gs and Fw 190 A-6s. These small numbers of German fighters were unable to protect the ground forces from Allied bombers and fighters bombers. The daylight raids by the 8th and 15th USAAF and night raids by the Royal Air Force became ever more intensive. Rumania was lost and Bulgaria had to be abandoned. The 6th German Army which had already been decimated at Stalingrad suffered the same fate south of Kishinev. On September 11 the American troops in the west were near Trier and the British reached the frontiers of the German Reich from Holland and Belgium. The Arnhem landings were a dreadful disaster for the Allies. Working together, SS troops and ground attack and fighter aircraft destroyed the British Airborne Division which had landed at Arnhem. But the Allied bomber formations and fighter bombers were uncontested masters of German air space. The German fighter groups grew smaller and smaller. It was only very occasionally that a Bf 109 or an Fw 190 managed to penetrate the escort fighters and gain access to the bombers. Usually, they were shot down by a Mustang or Thunderbolt as soon as they tried.

October 16 saw the largest American bomber formation operation so far in the eastern Mark. The main targets were the vehicle factories at Steyr and the tank factory at St. Valentin. Another formation attacked Salzburg. Smaller groups from this formation also attacked Graz and the airfield at Zeltweg. Fighter defence was strong but was shattered by the much smaller American formations. Oberst Handrick, Commander of the 8th Fighter Division which was responsible for this area, had virtually no formations of his own at this time. Only the night fighter aircraft were directly under his control. In an emergency fighter aircraft from other areas were allocated to him from I./JG 53. II./JG 52, III./JG 1, III./JG 3, III./JG 77 and fighter training school JG 108. To some extent JG 77, which was based in northern Italy and I./JG 4 helped to defend the eastern Mark. These aircraft were exclusively Bf 109 G-6s, G-10s and G-14s. When the improved P-47D and P-51D appeared in the summer of 1944 the chances of German fighters being successful were reduced even further day by day.

Although the Allies were hammering German aircraft factories with bombs, record fighter aircraft production figures were achieved in 1944. In 1943 6,247 Bf 109s had been built and in 1944 more than twice as many: 13,786. It is also certain that 11,767

Fw 190s were built. These cannot all be counted as fighters, however, as a large proportion of them were allocated to the ground attack formations. Also, 564 Me 262s had already been built but these could only be "by order of the Führer" initially and then only as "Blitzbombers". Nobody dared mention the Me 262 to him as a jet fighter. The Me 163 rocket fighter did not come up to expectations as a defence for fixed installations. And it couldn't be expected to do so as it was still virtually at an experimental stage. And there were only seven examples ever built of the revolutionary twin engine. Do 335 single-seat fighter. Fighter defence relied mainly on the Bf 109 because at altitude it was noticeably superior to the Fw 190 A with BMW 801 engine. It was only when the "long nose" Fw 190 D-9 with Jumo 213 appeared that the Fw 190 came to be feared by the Allied pilots. But they were too late and too few.

Meanwhile, at Hamburg-Finkenwerder, Dr. Vogt and his colleagues had developed the Me 155 to become the Bv 155. Following tests on a captured P-51 they had developed a new large span laminar flow wing on which large tunnel radiators had been added. The undercarriage borrowed the sprung legs of a Ju 87 D-6. Construction of the prototype Bv 155 V1 commenced at the beginning of 1944, and this aircraft was completed at the beginning of August and made its maiden flight on 1st September, 1944. This aircraft was powered by a DB 603 with TKL 15 supercharger but faults were discovered in the test flight programme with the result that Dr. Vogt decided to have a second prototype built, Bv 155 V2. But as construction was delayed time after time by repeated air raids the Bv 155 V2 could not be completed before 1945.

By the summer of 1944, General der

Jagdflieger Galland had assembled a fighter reserve of approximately 800 aircraft. When the western front started tottering this reserve was transferred senselessly in support of retreating German troops. A large proportion of the aircraft were directed to airfields which had already been surrendered and had to be blown up or fell into the hands of the British or Americans immediately because the airfields to which they had been ordered to fly had already been taken. In the confused situation, hundreds landed out in the fields and couldn't take off again. Over half were lost in this confusion without the slightest success. The normal western fighter formations reached the Rhine in a pretty poor state and the front line was stabilised here again. Their extremely low morale made a general re-grouping urgently necessary.

Once again, Galland set about creating a reserve. He dreamed of delivering a great blow for the defence of the Reich and inflicting decisive losses on the enemy bomber formations. He had in mind a massed formation of 2,000 to 3,000 fighters. And in fact towards the middle of November there were 18 fighter groups standing ready with 3,700 aircraft and pilots. The "great blow" had been carefully planned down to the last detail – but it never happened. There were two reasons: firstly the weather and secondly Hitler had thought of something different: the fighter reserve was to be prepared for action at the critical turning point in the west. He would not hear that most young fighter pilots were only trained to a level to fit them for flying defending the Reich. They would have needed at least some practice for the very different conditions on the front line. Apart from the fact that no aviation fuel was available, a change of that sort couldn't be carried out in a fortnight, and this applied to ground organisation as well. But the first postings were ordered for 20 November.

Operation "Wacht am Rhein" (Watch on the Rhine), the Ardennes Offensive, was aimed at the weakest point in the American lines, the 1st US Army under Lieutenant-General Hodges. Head of Luftwaffe Commando West, Generalleutnant Schmid had at his command a strong air force formation of 40 reconnaissance aircraft, 171 bombers, 91 ground attack aircraft and 1,492 fighters. To coincide with the beginning of the attack on 16 December 1944 V-1 (Fi 103) and V-2 (A 4) flying bombs and rockets were launched towards Antwerp and Lieges. It was to no avail as Allied air superiority precluded any chance of German success. In eight days British and American forces flew 6,000 missions! When the attack had run out of steam on 24 December 1944 1,088 German aircraft, most of them fighters, had been destroyed.

"Operation Bodenplatte" was the conclusion to this, an operation born of sheer despair. At dawn on New Year's Day, 1945, all the remaining fighter aircraft took off for a large scale carefully planned attack on Allied bases in northern France, Belgium and Holland. "Operation Bodenplatte" succeeded in destroying 400 enemy aircraft on the ground but these losses were hardly of any significance whatsoever as the Allies were in a position to replace them very quickly. But the German fighter service lost a further 3,000 fighter pilots, 59 of them formation leaders.

That was the first day of 1945.

Bf 109 G-14 of JG/54

The Galland cockpit
cover which was
fitted to all versions
of G-10 and after.
(Message on
fuselage side:
beware of front
rubber seal when
closing cockpit cover)

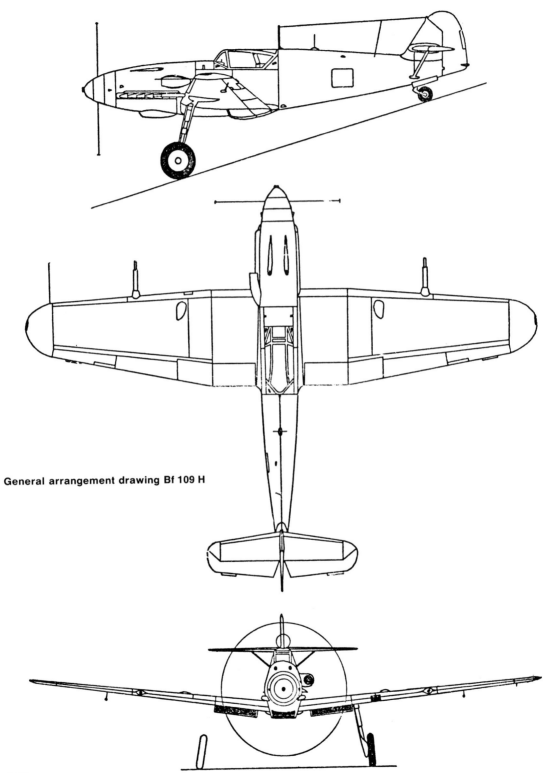

General arrangement drawing Bf 109 H

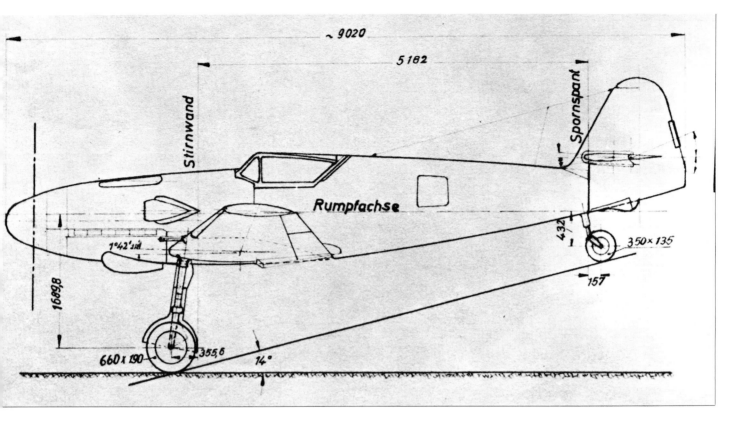

Side view Bf 109 H

Armament arrangement Bf 109 H

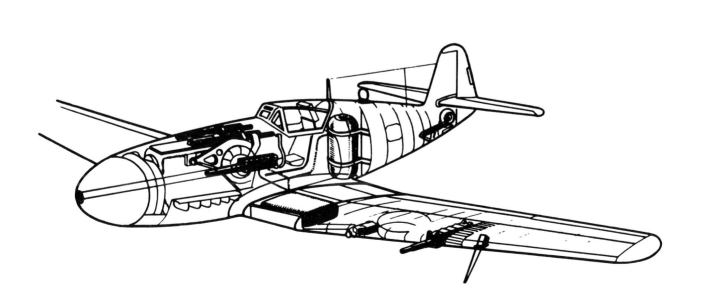

Bf 109 G-14 of JG 53 shot down

Bf 109 G-14, VD 358 at Farnborough, 1946

Bf 109 G-16 in the United States

11. The Fight to the Bitter End 1945

Although everyone knew that the war was lost, bitter fighting continued at the front and work in the factories continued with just as much determination. Aircraft manufacturers' design teams were generally dispersed in small villages. But the Allied fighter bombers were now not just attacking towns, refineries and factories — from now on anything that moved on the ground would be shot at.

It was in these difficult circumstances that Messerschmitt produced the last versions of the Bf 109. January 1945 saw the first Bf 109 K-6s coming off the assembly line. This version was designed specially for attacking large bombers. It had a pressurized cabin and was usually equipped with the MK 103 motor cannon. Above the engine, as in previous versions, were two MG 131s. A 300 litre extended range drop tank (field modification kit R3) and the addition of the two MK 108s (field mod. kit R5) were both possible. Fighter bomber missions using field modification kit R1 were rare. It was powered by the DB 605DCM with MW 50 injection system. It was only a short series. Equally only a few examples of the Bf 109 K-8, a fighter reconnaissance aircraft, saw service. This aircraft had a pressurized cabin too. Its armament consisted of 1 MK 103 motor cannon and two MK 108s in the wings. Like the K-6 the K-8 also had a

BSK 16 Robot camera in the leading edge of the wing. There were facilities for carrying 300 litre drop tanks. Using the MW 50 injection system, the aircraft had a maximum air speed of 441mph. In April 1945, Bf 109 K-10s and K-14s were still being produced and put into service. The K-10 differed from the K-6 very little. Equipment and armament were the same as the K-6 and it was powered by the DB 605D-1. Only two K-14s armed with three MK 108s were delivered. This version, powered by a DB 605L with 1750 PS, had a speed of 452mph. It was the fastest Bf 109.

On February 8 1945 the Bv 155 V2 took off on its maiden flight. It had a larger tail than the V1 and had benefited from a number of structural changes. But after a few test flights it nosed over when landing on soft ground.

The aircraft was not too badly damaged and would have been worth repairing. The construction of the third prototype Bv 155 V3 dragged on. The aircraft was very similar to its V2 predecessor but had the DB 603U engine with TKL 15 supercharger. About 15th March 1945, Dr. Vogt submitted to the Technisches Amt a new design of the Bv 155, the Bv 155 C, which represented a radical change from the original design. Although Germany was on the verge of total collapse, the Technisches Amt ordered the

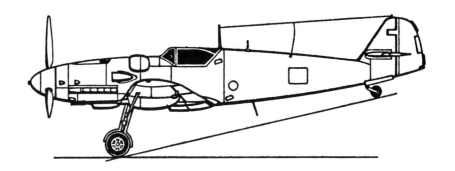

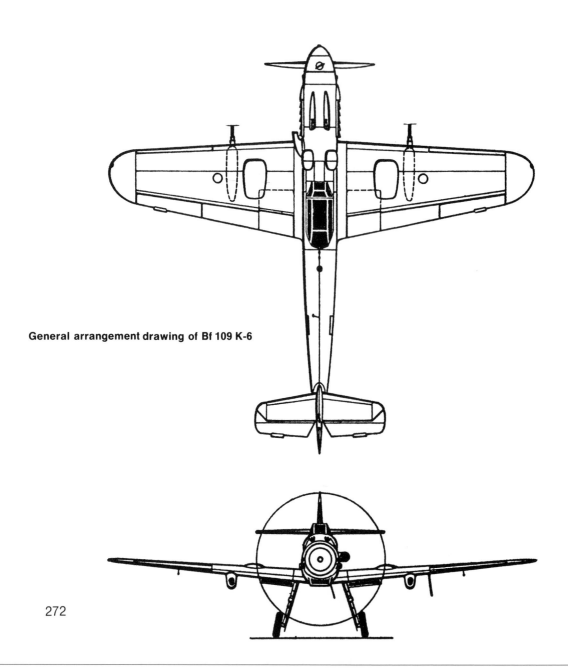

General arrangement drawing of Bf 109 K-6

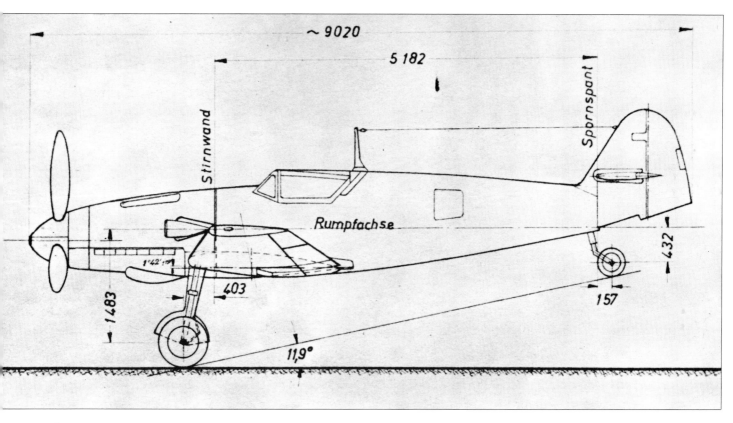

Side view of Bf 109 K

Armament arrangement Bf 109 K-6

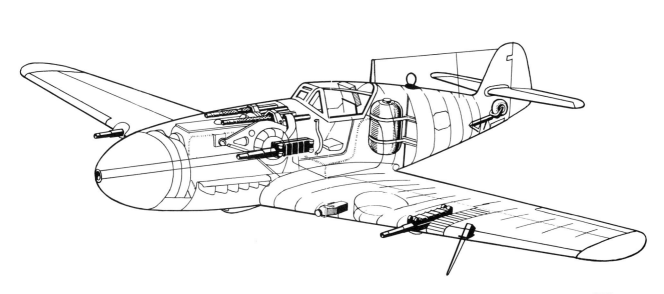

273

Bf 109 K-2 of I/JG 51 at Zatek airfield, Czechoslovakia, May 1945

This is how the Allies found the Bv 155 V3

Bf 109 K-4 of
II./NJG 11

The underwing radiator
of the Bv 155 V3

This photograph
shows that there was
little of the original
Me 155 design left

275

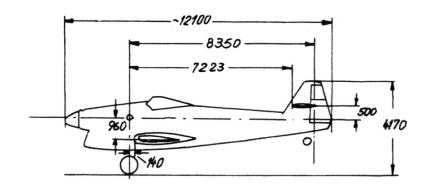

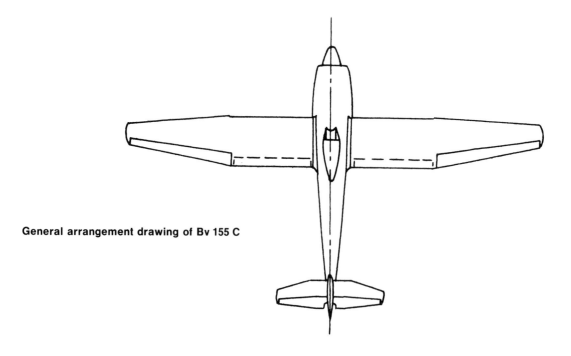

General arrangement drawing of Bv 155 C

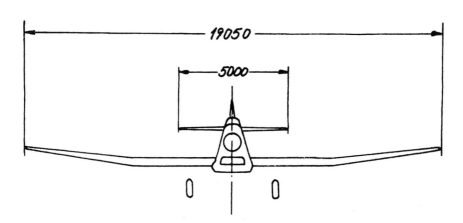

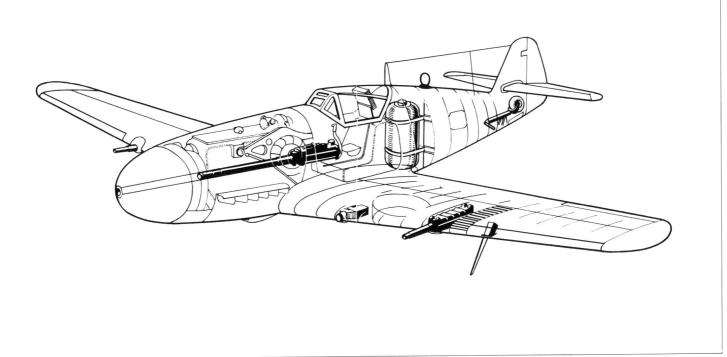

Armament arrangement Bf 109 K-8

Engine and armament installation Bf 109 K-10

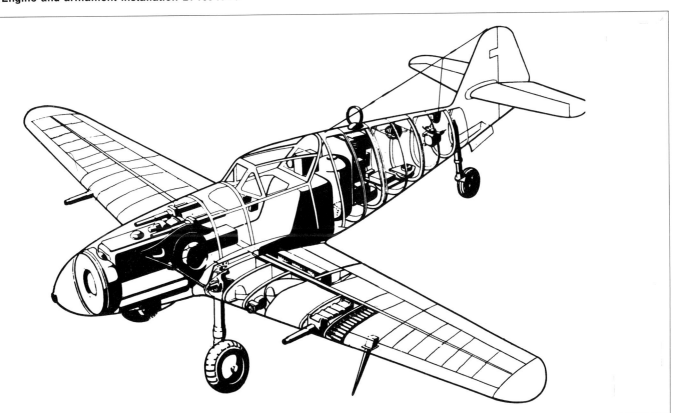

construction of 3 prototypes V4 and V6 also 30 Bv 155 C-0 series aircraft. It is unlikely that any of these concerned could seriously imagine this contract being completed.

All that was left of the Bv 155 was the incomplete Bv 155 V3 discovered by English troops in May 1945 at Hamburg-Finkenwerder and immediately transported to Farnborough for further tests. From there it was taken to the United States and designated FE 505 (FE = Foreign Equipment). It is possible that the components of this aircraft are still in the National Air and Space Museum in Washington D.C.

After Hitler had given his last radio speech on 30 January, 1945 in which he called on everyone to fight on there was a major air raid on the next day when the 15th USAAF attacked the fuel installations of Donau/Chemie at Mossbierbaum with 217 B-17s and 407 B-24s whilst tactical bomber formations attacked the Brenner railway so ferociously that the supplies for German formations in northern Italy were interrupted for almost a week. Most of the few remaining serviceable German fighters on the airfields at Graz and Klagenfurt were eliminated in low level attacks by American single-seat fighters. Lockheed P-38s destroyed numerous Bf 109 G-10s on those airfields.

On February 3rd, 1945 there was again a heavy air raid on Berlin by the 8th USAAF with 937 bombers and 613 fighter aircraft. Using desperate tactics, a few Bf 109s and Fw 190s, flew into the formations and shot down 26 B-17s and 8 escort fighters.

In the middle of February there was the notorious RAF and 8th USAAF air raid on Dresden. German supply routes were systematically destroyed. On March 24 the 21st Allied Army Group, under Field Marshal Montgomery, crossed the Lower Rhine at Wesel. On the next day the whole of the Palatinate was in the hands of the Allies. On April 4 the last of the German troops evacuated Hungary. The Russians were already deep into East Prussia and Pomerania. On April 29 1945 the southern front capitulated. The last Luftwaffe mission in Austria, previously the "Eastern Mark", was carried out by Fw 190s of the Schlachtgeschwader 10 (ground attack) on 4 May 1945. The following day the airfields at Linz and Hörsching were taken by the Americans after the German fighters had already taken off. On April 15 Soviet forces surrounded Berlin. On the afternoon of 30 April 1945 Hitler committed suicide. On May 7 at 2.41 the capitulation of the German forces was signed at Rheims. The war was over.

Bf 109 G-10/U3 of II./JG 11 at the end of the war

The Bf 109 G-6s delivered to Switzerland

Wrecked Bf 109s, Prag-Rusin 1945

Time to leave Norway: Norwegian soldiers with Bf 109 wrecks and other German aircraft at Bardufoss

12. Did any Bf 109s Survive?

The story of the Luftwaffe was at an end. But that of the Bf 109 was far from finished. Before and during the war Bf 109s had been supplied to Finland, Rumania, Hungary and Switzerland. In the Winter of 1938/39 Switzerland had taken delivery of ten D-1s, but the Swiss Kommando der Flieger wanted the more powerful E-3, so between April 1939 and April 1940, 80 Bf 109 E-3s were delivered to Switzerland and allocated to Fliegerkompagnie 6, 7, 8, 9, 15 and 21. These were used quite ruthlessly by the Swiss to maintain their neutrality. As British and American bombers often deviated across Switzerland pursued by German night fighters when returning from a mission, it sometimes happened that the Swiss were fighting not just Allied bombers but also German heavy fighters in pursuit. So Swiss Bf 109s sometimes shot down German Bf 110s!

Only two examples of the F-4 series were delivered to Switzerland. On 29 March 1944 a Bf 109 G landed at Samaden and was immediately captured by Swiss air force personnel. On 28 April 1944 Hauptmann Wilhelm Johnen of the III./NJG 6 flying a Bf 110 G-4b was forced to land in Dübendorf after pursuing a Lancaster over Swiss territory. His aircraft had the latest radar equipment on board: FuG 220 Lichtenstein SN 2 and FuG 350 Naxos Z, a device for homing in on the H2S Allied navigational radar. The Allied secret service in Switzerland would probably have got their hands on this equipment. At first there were plans to take the aircraft by force and destroy it, but the Swiss would not have been pleased. There were negotiations and a rather unusual deal was agreed: twelve new Bf 109 G-6s would be supplied to Switzerland in return for the destruction of the Bf 110 G-4b. And that was what happened in May 1944. The Bf 109 was still in service in Switzerland up to the end of 1949, but then they had to be taken out of service through lack of spare parts. There is still a well cared for Bf 109 E-3 in the Swiss Transport Museum (Verkehrsmuseum) in Lucerne.

During the war an export version Bf 109 J had been devised for the Spanish. They took delivery of 25 Bf 109 G-2 airframes which were to serve as the model for licensed construction. The deal did not include power units, so the Spanish were forced to fit other engines. Hispano Aviacion SA did not have a wide choice of engines available and used the licence-built Hispano-Suiza HS 12Z 89 which produced 1300PS. As this V12 engine was not of inverted arrangement it did not fit into the airframe as easily as the DB 605. The 25 machines were completed and designated HA-1.109 J. But their performance was never equal to that of the

The end in Berlin: Shot up Bf 109 K at Hasenheide near Tempelhof airport

Bf 109 G-10 of the Finnish Air Force, at Kuopio

Hispano-Aviacion HA
1109-K-1-L

HA 1109-K-1-L with
experimental
wing-mounted cannon

HA 1109-K-1-L with
new cannon
arrangement

283

The Hispano-Suiza motor produced some unusual cowling arrangements

Opposite top to bottom:
HA 1110 K-1-L
HA 1112 C 4-K-43
HA 1112 M-4-L

Centre: HA 1109-K-3-L Bottom: Prototype HA 1109-M-1-L

Above: HA 1112-M-1-L. Below: A Spanish Bf 109 representing a German fighter of I./JG27 in the film about Hans-Joachim Marseille

Bf 109 G-2 on which they were based. In the meantime the Spanish had started to manufacture airframes. There were tests with the Hispano-Suiza HS 12Z 17 and various armament arrangements and these led to a new version, HA-1109-K1L. An improved HA-1109-K3L version was fitted with eight 80mm Oerlikon rockets. In 1954 the first HA-1109-K1L was fitted with two Breda-Safat 12.7mm machine guns. The Hispano-Suiza motor was underpowered and the replacement engine selected was the Rolls-Royce Merlin 500-45. The prototype of this new version HA-1109-MIL flew in 1954 and went into series production. These aircraft were still flying with the Spanish Air Force in 1959. Two of the HA-1109-K1Ls were converted in 1953 to two-seater fighter trainers HA-1110-K1L. They were later fitted with the Merlin engine and redesignated HA-1112-M4L. During the production of a German film on Hans-Joachim Marseille the Spanish HA 1112-M1L (the series version of HA 1109-M1L) flew with the markings of 1. Gruppe of the German JG 27 and brought back memories of the battles of 1942/43. The last Spanish Bf 109 went out of service in 1967. In the closing years of the war Bf 109 G-12s and G-14s were assembled from parts in Czechoslovakia (Bohemia & Moravia as it was known at that time). After the defeat of Germany, Avia continued building both types as C-10 (Bf 109 G-14) and C 110 (G-12). The Czech Air Force flew them as S 99 and CS 99 respectively.

Production of both Bf 109 versions was transferred a short time later to the firm Letov at Letmany near Prague. From 1943 Letov had been involved in producing components for the Ju 88. Twenty S 99s and two CS 99s were built at Letov. Then all remaining DB 605AS engines which had been stored in an ammunition dump were destroyed in a fire. The choice of replacement engine was limited to a number of older Jumo 211F engines which had been stored as spares for the repair of He 111s in Czechoslavakia. And so it happened that Bf 109 airframes were fitted with this bomber engine and underwent the necess-

Messerschmitt by Hispano-Aviacion. Overview of the HA versions

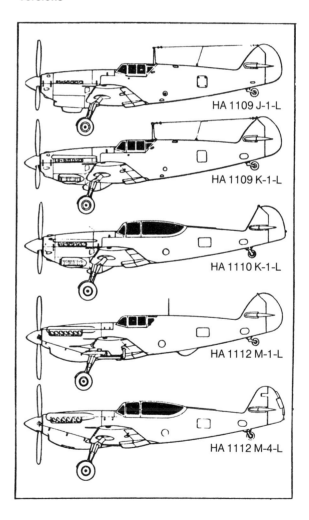

HA 1109 J-1-L

HA 1109 K-1-L

HA 1110 K-1-L

HA 1112 M-1-L

HA 1112 M-4-L

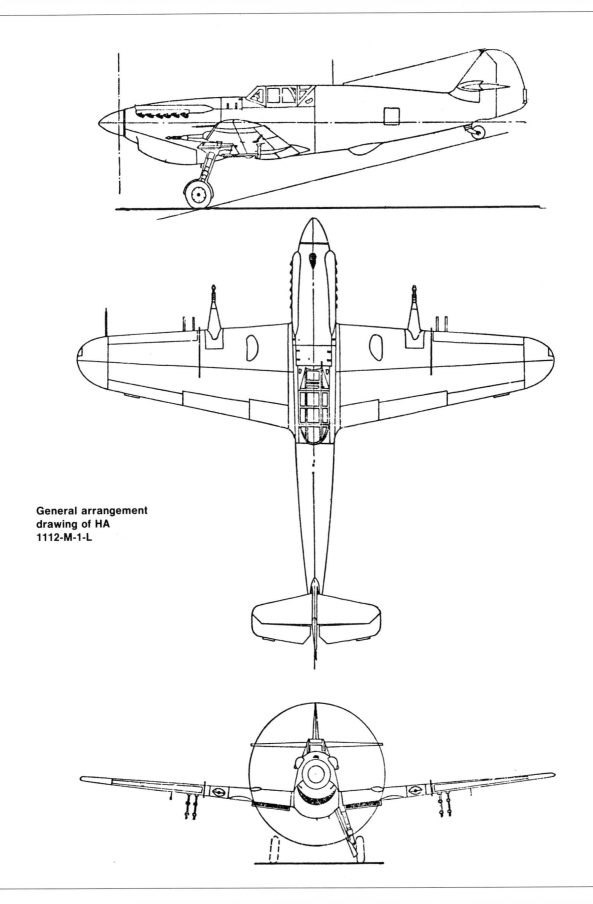

**General arrangement
drawing of HA
1112-M-1-L**

Bf 109 G-14 = Avia S 99 (above). Fighter trainer Avia CS 99 (below).

Below: Avia S 199

ary major changes to the engine cowling. The Junkers VS11 propellers used on the Jumo 211F were also fitted. The characteristic shape of the Bf 109 G was retained, whereas the Spanish Bf 109 looked different. The Czech Bf 109s produced in this way were designated C 210 and C 210 C and the Czech Air Force flew them as S 199 and CS 199. It is likely that the combination of the lightweight airframe with the heavy bomber engine and propellor left much to be desired – the Jumo was about 40kg heavier than the DB 605. The pilots didn't like the difficult handling of this aircraft very much and referred to it as the "Maulesel" (donkey). Surprisingly in this form the Bf 109 was to do battle once again. Threatened by its Arab neighbours the young state of Israel tried to buy fighter planes all over the world but was rejected. Only Czechoslovakia made an offer, namely of their S 199s. Under the cloak of secrecy the Israeli Air Force, Chel Ha'avir, bought 25 S 199s for $190,000- each. These aircraft were transferred under the operation codename "Balak". They were used to set up the first Israeli fighter unit, the 10th Squadron under the command of Modi Alon in 1948. When war broke out against Palestine Bf 109s and Spitfires were in each other's gunsights once again. The old Bf 109 showed that despite all its faults it hadn't forgotten much and many an Egyptian Spitfire was brought down by an S 199. Nowadays there is just one of these 25 aircraft maintained for historic reasons on an Israeli airfield, a reminder of these first Jewish fighter aircraft with Nazi origins.

There is no shortage of proof that over 40

Avia S 199, showing the installation of the Jumo 211

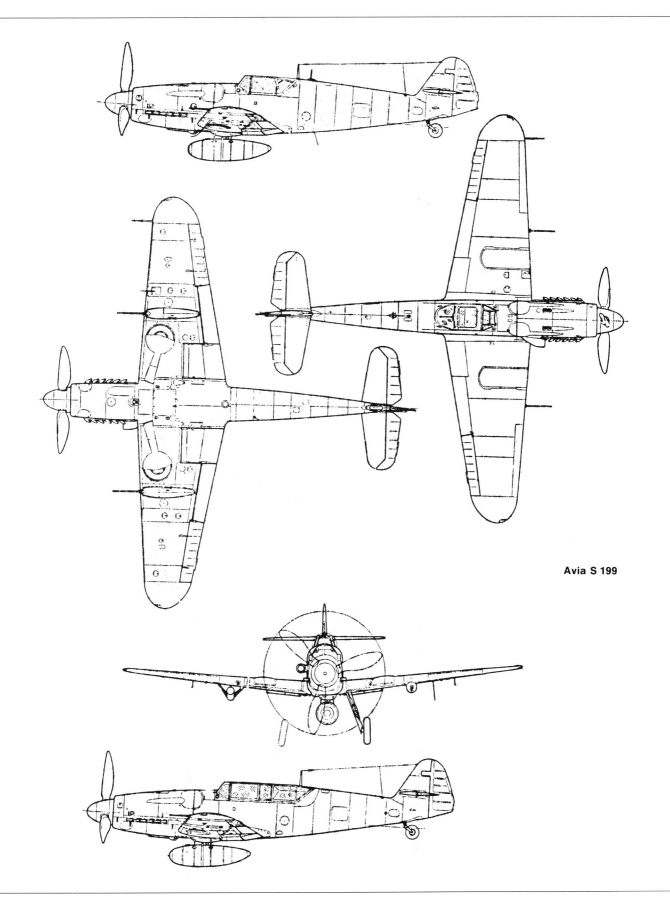

Avia S 199

A Czech pilot landed
in the Federal
Republic of Germany
in the S 199 and
handed over the
aircraft to the
Americans

Two of the S 199
delivered to Israel by
Czechoslovakia

292

Avia CS 199 fighter trainer after a crash landing

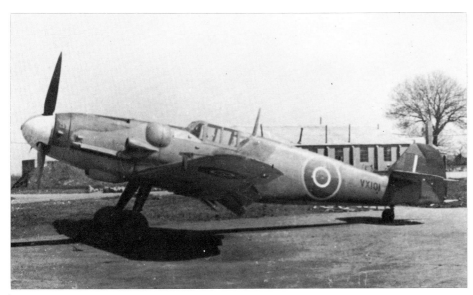

A Bf 109 G-6 at Farnborough, captured by the British

This Bf 109 G-6/R6/U4 of I./JG 11 was also captured by the British

293

years after the end of the Second World War the Messerschmitt Bf 109 is far from forgotten. In all the model aircraft magazines both in Germany and elsewhere there are detailed plans and instructions including paint schemes and fighter unit markings or personal emblems of famous German fighter pilots. There are Bf 109s all over the world, some wrecks, and Bf 109 enthusiasts are restoring the aircraft with loving care and spending vast amounts of time and money to return them to their former glory.

There is considerable activity in the USA. There is a Bf 109 G-6 in the National Air and Space Museum, Washington. Considerable care has been taken over the restoration there of the aircraft which was stored for many years at O'Hare Airport, Illinois. All markings had been removed and there was no indication as to the origin of the aircraft. In 1948 the aircraft was transferred in component form to Washington. After searching through hundreds of photos it was decided that the paint scheme and markings of Bf 109 G-6/R3, no. 2 of III. Gruppe of JG 27 would be appropriate. Works no. 160 163 was painted on the tail, also taken from the photograph. When the new building of the National Air and Space Museum was opened on 4 July 1976 this Bf 109 was one of the main attractions for visitors, and still is.

There is a G-14/R3 in Buena Park, California (works no. 611 943). There is a G-10 being restored in the private air museum of Ontario, California, and in Sun Valley, also in California, a G-14. In Dayton, Ohio, the USAF Museum is shortly to display a Spanish HA-1112-M1L in German markings. The so-called "Confederate Air Force" also has a Spanish HA-1112-M1L in flying condition but in the markings of III./JG 52.

In England there is an E-6 of 4./JG 26 in Bournemouth which is to be restored. There is an excellently restored E-4 of 2./JG 51 at St. Athan in Wales, and there is a G-2 *trop.*, works no. 10639, at RAF Lyneham in Wiltshire. There are probably other Bf 109s stored in packing cases at Farnborough. In Finland there are two well-kept G-10 *trop.*, MT 452 and MT 507, at Utti and Rissala airfields. There is an E-3 and an F-4 *trop.*, both well restored, in the South African National War Museum. And the E-3 in the Swiss Transport Museum in Lucerne has already been mentioned.

Even in Australia there is a Bf 109 G-10 (works no. 163824) and it is in good condition. It arrived at the Royal Air Force Airbase at Laverton by military transport and in the mid-Sixties was sold to a Mr Sidney Marshall in Bankstown as "war surplus", and he restored the aircraft in detail with loving care. And in Germany? There is a Bf 109 E-3 works no. 790 in the Deutsches Museum, Munich. It is in excellent condition but the camouflage is not entirely correct. Otherwise there are only Spanish licence-built aircraft in Germany: one of them at a small airfield at Fiegen bears the colours and markings of III./JG 54; another in the markings of II./JG 2 is in the Luftwaffe Museum in Utersen, and there is a similar aircraft at the new Messerschmitt factory in Augsburg.

At the Technische Hochschule in Aachen, work is proceeding to convert a Spanish HA 1112-M1L back to a German Bf 109 G by fitting a German DB 605 engine. So there is no risk that the most numerous German fighter of World War II will be forgotten, a fate it shares with the best German fighter of World War I, the Fokker D VII.

The Me 209 V1, which once made history, is still in existence, though dismantled. It is in the Polish National Air Museum in Cracow. The mystery as to how it got there

Bf 109 G-10/U4 at Maloney's Air Museum, Ontario, California

Bf 109 K-4 in 1946 at an airfield in Maryland U.S.A.

Avia CS 199 in the Museum in Prague-Kbely

295

is easily solved: it was transferred to Poland with many old German aircraft from the aircraft collection at Lehrter station in Berlin to protect it from destruction in the air raids. There, like Udet's Curtiss Hawk and other historical aircraft, some of which are from the period before 1914, it is quietly rotting. No-one in West Germany has yet taken an interest in the fate of these aircraft.

It is uncertain how many old Bf 109s still exist in the East, though the author is aware of one in Belgrade and one in Poland.

The remains of the Me 209 V1 in the Museum at Krakow Poland

13. How many Messerschmitt 109s were actually built?

There has been uncertainty about the number of Bf 109s built in Germany and under licence. Many different figures have been put forward. The following figures are based on intensive research both here and abroad and can be regarded as accurate:

Pre-war	1076
From the outbreak of war to the end of 1939	449
1940	1693
1941	2764
1942	2665
1943	6247
1944	13786
1945	2969
Total	31649*
Czechoslovakia	573
Spain	239
Total	32461

* In this figure are included 25 airframes (without engine) delivered to Spain

Bf 109 H Projected Developments

Me P 1091

Me 109 H V55

Me 209 H V1

Bf 109 E-4 fitted experimentally with over-wing aerodynamic fuel tanks

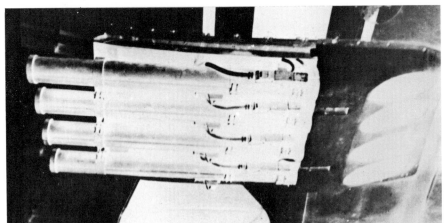

RZ65 rocket launchers under the wing of Bf 109 F-2, works no. 9246

Bf 109 F-2, works no. 9246 with eight RZ65

298

The only remaining
photographs of the
V-tail Bf 109 G-03,
Works no. 14003,
VJ + WC

Appendices

Side view drawings of the main versions of the Bf 109

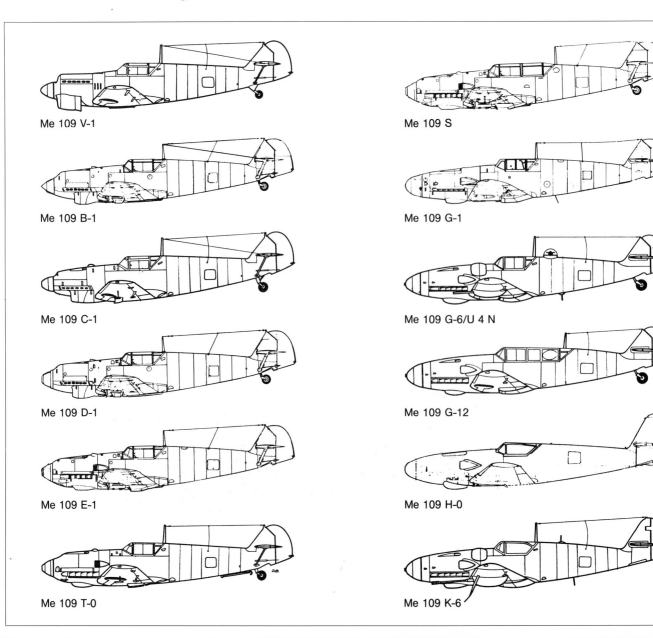

Me 109 V-1

Me 109 S

Me 109 B-1

Me 109 G-1

Me 109 C-1

Me 109 G-6/U 4 N

Me 109 D-1

Me 109 G-12

Me 109 E-1

Me 109 H-0

Me 109 T-0

Me 109 K-6

Messerschmitt Bf 109 – Me 609

Experimental Aircraft, Prototypes and Projects

Type	Year	Engine	PS	Registration/ possible modifications	Works no. or comments
Bf 109 V1	1935	RR-Kestrel	695	D-IABI	758 Series A
Bf 109 V2	1935	Jumo 210 A	640	D-IDUE	759 Series A
Bf 109 V3	1935	Jumo 210 A	640	D-IOQY	760 Series A
Bf 109 V4	1935	Jumo 210 Da	650	D-IALY	878 B-01
Bf 109 V5	1936	Jumo 210 Da	650	D-IEKS (D-IIGO?)	879 B-02
Bf 109 V6	1936	Jumo 210 Da	650	D-IHHB	880 B-03
Bf 109 V7	1936	Jumo 210 Ga	720	D-IJHA	881 B-04 = C
Bf 109 V8	1936	Jumo 210 Ga	720	D-IPLU	882 B-05 = C
Bf 109 V9	1937	Jumo 210 Ga	720	Zürich 37	883 B-06
Bf 109 V10	1937	Jumo 210 Ga	720	Zürich 37	884 B-07
Bf 109 B-1	1937	Jumo 210 Da	650	Wooden Propeller 2 MG 17	Short Series
Bf 109 B-2	1937	Jumo 210 Ea/G	680	Metal Propeller 3 MG 17	Series
Bf 109 C-1	1937	Jumo 210 Ga	720	Metal Propeller 4 MG 17	Series
Bf 109 C-2	1938	Jumo 210 Ga	720	Metal Propeller 5 MG 17	Short Series
Bf 109 C-3	1938	Jumo 210 Ga	720	2 MG 17, 2 MG/FF	Test Aircraft Only
Bf 109 C-4	1938	Jumo 210 Ga	720	4 MG 17, MG/FFM	Test Aircraft Only
Bf 109 V11	1938	DB 600 A	910	Unarmed	B-08 = D
Bf 109 V12	1938	DB 600 A	910	Unarmed	B-09 = D
Bf 109 D-1	1938	Jumo 210 D	680	4 MG 17	Long Series
Bf 109 V13	1937	DB 600 A	1650	Record: Dr. Wurster D-IPKY	B-010 = E-01
Bf 109 V14	1937	DB 600 A	910	D-ISLU	
Bf 109 V15	1938	DB 601 A-1	1100	D-IPHR	E-03 = E-1
Bf 109 V16	1938	DB 601 A-1	1100	D-IPGS	E-04 = E-1
Bf 109 V17	1938	DB 601 A-1	1100	D-IWKU	E-05 = E-1
Bf 109 V18	1938	DB 601 A-1	1100	D-ITXP	E-06 = E-1
Bf 109 E-1	1939	DB 601 A-1	1100	4 MG 17	Series
Bf 109 E-1B	1939	DB 601 A-1	1100	4 MG 17, 250kg Bomb	1. Bf 109-Jabo (fighter bomber)
Bf 109 V20	1938/9	DB 601 A-1	1100	CE + BM	E-08 = E-2 W.Nr. 5601
Bf 109 E-2	1939	DB 601 A-1	1100	2 MG 17 + 3 MG/FF	
Bf 109 V19	1938/9	DB 601 A-1	1100	D-IRTT	E-07 = E-3
Bf 109 E-3	1940	DB 601 Aa	1175	2 MG 17 + 2 MG/FF (+ R1?)	Long Series
Bf 109 E-4	1940	DB 601 Aa	1175	as E-3, also trop and R1	Long Series
Bf 109 E-5	1940/41	DB 601 A-1	1100	2 MG 17, Rb 21/18	Fighter Reconnaissance
Bf 109 E-6	1941	DB 601 N	1175	2 MG 17, Rb 21/18 (+ R3?)	Fighter Reconnaissance
Bf 109 E-7	1941	DB 601 A-1	1100	2 MG 17, 2 MG/FF R1, R3, GM1	Fighter Bomber and Fighter
Bf 109 E-8	1941	DB 601 E	1350	as E-7	
Bf 109 E-9	1941	DB 601 E	1350	2 MG 17, Rb 50/30, R3	Fighter Reconnaissance
Bf 109 T-0	1939/40	DB 601 Aa-1	1175	2 MG 17 + 2 MG/FF	Converted from 10 E-3 at Fieseler
Bf 109 T-1	1940/41	DB 601 Aa-1	1175	as T-0	60 built, converted to T-2
Bf 109 T-2	1942	DB 601 N	1175	as T-0 R1, R3	
Bf 109 V21	1940	DB 601 A-1	1100	Ce + BN	E-09 = F-0 W.Nr. 6502
Bf 109 V22	1940	DB 601 A-1	1100	D-IRRQ = CE + BO	E-010 = F-0 W.Nr. 1800

Messerschmitt Bf 109 – Me 609
Experimental Aircraft, Prototypes and Projects

Type	Year	Engine	PS	Registration/ possible modifications	Works no. or comments
Bf 109 V23	1940	DB 601 E-1	1350	CE + BP	= F-0 W.Nr. 5603
Bf 109 V24	1940	DB 601 E-1	1350	VK + AB	= F-0 W.Nr. 5604
Bf 109 F-0	1940/41	DB 601 N	1175	2 MG 17 + 1 MG/FFM, R1, R3	
Bf 109 F-1	1941	DB 601 N	1175	as F-0	Series
Bf 109 F-2	1941	DB 601 N	1175	2 MG 17 + 1 MG 151/15, R1, R3, *trop*, GM1	Series
Bf 109 F-3	1941	DB 601 E	1350	2 MG 17 + 1 MG 151/20, R1, R3, *trop*, GM1	Series
Bf 109 F-4	1942	DB 601 E	1350	as F-3, R1, R3, R5, R6, *trop*	Series
Bf 109 F-5	1942	DB 601 E	1350	2 MG 17, R3, Rb 50/30	Fighter Reconnaissance
Bf 109 F-6	1942	DB 601 E	1350	Unarmed, R3, Rb 50/30	Fighter Reconnaissance
Bf 109 V25 bis V29				No information, probably pre-tests for G series	
Bf 109 G-01	1941	DB 601 E	1350	2 MG 17 + 1 MG 151/20	VJ + WA, W.Nr. 14001
Bf 109 G-02	1941/42	DB 601 E	1350	as G-01	Pre-series: 12 aircraft
Bf 109 G-03	1943	DB 601 E	1350	as G-01	V-Tailplane, W.Nr. 14003
Bf 109 G-1	1942	DB 605 A-1	1475	as G-01 Pressurized Cabin	Series
Bf 109 G-1 trop	1942	DB 605 A-1	1475	2 MG 131, 1 MG 151/20, Pressurized Cabin, *trop*	
Bf 109 G-2	1942	DB 605 A-1	1475	2 MG 17 + 1 WT 17, R3, Rb 50/30 Fighter Reconnaissance without Pressurized Cabin	
Bf 109 G-3	1942	DB 605 A-1	1475	2 MG 17 + 1 MG 151/20, FuG 16 Z, R1, R3, pressurized Cabin	
Bf 109 G-4	1942	DB 605 A-1	1475	2 MG 17 + 1 MG 151/20	as G-3 but without Pressurized Cabin
Bf 109 G-5	1942/43	DB 605 A/AS	1475	2 MG 131 + 1 Mg 151/20, R1, R2, R3,, U2, Pressurized Cabin, some with GM 1	
Bf 109 G-6	1942–44	DB 605 div. Versionen	1475	2 MG 131 + 1 MG 151/20 or MK 108, without Pressurized Cabin, U2, U4, R1, 2, 3, 5, 6, 7, *trop*, N	
Bf 109 G-7	1943			equivalent to G-6/U4	No Series Production
Bf 109 G-8	1943	DB 605 A-1/AS	1475	1 MG 151/20, Rb 12.5/7, or 32/7 x 9, Robot li, U2, U3, R1, 2, 3, 5, 6, 7	
Bf 109 G-10	1944	DB 605 A/D	1435	2 MG 131 + 1 MK 108, R1, 2, 3, 5, 6, 7	
Bf 109 G-10	1944	DB 605 A/D	1435	2 MG 131 + 1 Mk 108, R1, 2, 3, 5, 6, 7, U2, U4	
Bf 109 V52	1942/43	DB 605 A-1	1475	CJ + MG	Works no. 18319 = G-12
Bf 109 G-12	1943	DB 605 A-1	1475	2 MG 17	Two-seater Fighter Trainer
Bf 109 G-14	1944	DB 605 AM/AS	1435	2 MG 131 + 1 MG 151/20, R1, 3, 6, 7, U2, U4	
Bf 109 G16	194/45	DB 605 D	1435	as G-14, R1, 6, 7	

Messerschmitt Bf 109 – Me 609 — Experimental Aircraft, Prototypes and Projects

Type	Year	Engine	PS	Registration/ possible modifications	Works no. or comments
Bf 109 V54	1943	DB 628	1475	Unarmed	DV + JB W.Nr. 15708 = H
Bf 109 H-0	1943	DB 601 E-1	1350	2MG 17 + 1 MK 108 Rb 20/30, 50/30 or 75/30, GM 1	Converted from Me 109 F
Bf 109 H-1	1944	DB 605 A-1	1475	2 MG 17 + 1 MG 151/20, GM 1	Converted from G-5
Bf 109 H-2	Proj	Jumo 213 E	1750	2 MG 131 + 3 MK 108, GM 1	High Altitude Fighter
Bf 109 H-3	Proj	Jumo 213 E	1750	GM 1, Rb 50/30 or 75/30	High Altitude Reconnaissance
Bf 109 H-4	Proj	Jumo 213 E	1750	3 MK 108, 500kg Bomb	High Altitude Fighter Bomber
Bf 109 H-5	Proj	DB 605 L	1475	3 MK 108 + 2 MG 131	High Altitude Fighter
Bf 109 K-0	1944	DB 605 D	1435	1 MK 108 + 2 MG 151/15, GM 1, U2, U4, U6, R4	
Bf 109 K-2	1944	DB 605 ASCM	1475		as K-0, but MW 50 instead of GM 1
Bf 109 K-4	1944	DB 605 div.	1435	1 MK 108 + 2 MG 131, Pressurized Cabin, R1, 3, 5, 6	
Bf 109 K-6	1944	DB 605 D-1	1435	as K-4, but either MK 103 or 108	
Bf 109 K-8	1944/45	DB 605 ASB	1475	2 MK 108 or MG 151/20, Pressurized Cabin, Rb 50/30 or 75/30, R3 Fighter Reconnaissance	
Bf 109 K-10	1945	DB 605 D-1	1435	1 MK 103 + 2 MG 131, Pressurized Cabin, R3, 4, 5	
Bf 109 K-14	1945	DB 605 L	1475	1 MK 103/108 + 2 MG 131, Pressurized Cabin, R3, 4, 5	
Bf 109 Z-0	1942/43	DB 601 E	2 x 1350	5 MG 151, ETC 250 NG + RS (2 x F-4)	
Bf 109 Z-2	Proj.	DB 605 A-1	2 x 1475	2 MK 108 + 1 MK 103 ETC 500	
Bf 109 Z-3	Proj.	Jumo 213 E	2 x 1750	4 MK 108 + 1 MK 103	
Bf 109 Z-4	Proj.	Jumo 213 E	2 x 1750	2 MK 108, 2000kg Bombs	
Bf 109S	Proj.	DB 601-A1	1100	2MG77	Two-seater Trainer from E-Series
Me 509	1943/44	Db 605B	2000	2 MG 131 + 2 MG 151	Engine behind Pilot
Me 155	Proj.1942	DB 605 A-1	1475	3 MG 151/20	
BF 109 V50	1943/44	DB 628	1475	Unarmed	Converted from G-3/R4 Works no. 15338
Me 155 B-1	Proj.1942	DB 628	1475	Various armament arrangements planned	
Me 155 B-1a	Proj.1943	DB 603 A	1750	Various armament arrangements planned	
Bv 155 V3	1945	DB 603 U	1750	Unarmed TKL 15	Test Aircraft
Bv 155 C	Proj.	DB 603 U	1750	Unarmed TKL 15	Test Aircraft
Me 209 V1	1938	DB 601 V10		World Record Aircraft	D-INJR W.Nr. 1185
Me 209 V2	1939	DB 601 A-1	1100		D-IWAH W.Nr. 1186
Me 209 V3	1939	DB 601 A-1	1100		D-IVFP W.Nr. 1187
Me 209 V4	1940	DB 601 N	1175	2 MG 17 + 1 MG/FFM	D-IRND W.Nr. 1188 later CE + BW

Messerschmitt Bf 109 – Me 609 **Experimental Aircraft, Prototypes and Projects**

Type	Year	Engine	PS	Registration/ possible modifications	Works no. or comments
Me 209 V5	1943/44	DB 603 G	2000	2 MG 131 + 2 MG 151/20	SP + LJ
Me 209 V6	1944	Jumo 213 E	1750	IMK 108 + 2 MG 151/20	later redesignated Bf 109 L
P.1091	Proj.1943	DB 632			High Altitude Fighter
BF 109 V49	Proj.1943	DB628	1475	Unarmed	Converted from G-5 W.Nr. 16291
Bf 109 V50	Proj.1943	DB 628	1475	Unarmed	Converted from G-5 W.Nr. 15338
Bf 109 V55	Proj.1943	DB 628	1475	Unarmed DV + JC	Converted from G-5 W.Nr. 15709
Me 209 HV1	Proj.1943	DB 603 G	2000	1 MK 108, 2 MG 131, 4 MG 151	Fate unknown
Bf 109 V23	1942	DB 601 E-1	1350	Unarmed (Me 109 Nosewheel)	CE + BP W.nr. 5603
Bf 109 V30	1942	DB 601 E-1	1350	Unarmed (Me 109 Nosewheel) Pressurized Cabin	ND + IE W.Nr. 5716
Bf 109 V3a	1942	DB 601 E-1	1350	Unarmed (Me 109 Nosewheel) Pressurized Cabin	ND + IF W.Nr. 5717
Bf 109 V31	1942	DB 601 E-1	1350	Unarmed (Me 109 Nosewheel)	SG + EK W.Nr. 5642
Me 309 V1	1942	DB 603 A-1	1750	Unarmed 1943 = DB 603 V4	GE + CU
Me 309 V2	1942/43	DB 605 B	2000	Unarmed Crashed 28.11.42	GE = CV
Me 309 V3	1943	DB 605 B	2000	Unarmed	GE + CW
Me 309 V4	1943	DB 605 B	2000	Weapon Tests	RH + LH
Me 409	1943/44	DB 603 G	2 x 2000	2 MK 108 + 3 MG 151	Converted from 2 Me 209 V5
Me 509	1943/44	DB 605 B	2000	2 MG 131 + 2 MG 151	Engine behind Pilot
Me 609	1943/44	DB 605 B	2 x 2000	4 MK 108 + 2 MK 103 500kg Bombs	Converted from 2 Me 309

Technical Data on the main Bf 109 Variants

Aircraft Type		Bf 109 V1 (a)	V3(A)	B-1	B-2
Year of Construction		1935	1936	1936	1936/37
Crew		1	1	1	1
Engine		RR-Kestrel V	Jumo 210 A	Jumo 210 D	Jumo 210 Da
Power	PS *	695	610	680	685
Wingspan	(m)	9.87	9.87	9.90	9.90
Length	(m)	8.58	8.58	8.70	8.70
Height	(m)	2.45	2.45	2.45	2.45
Wing Area	(m²)	16.17	16.17	16.35	16.35
Empty Weight	(kg)	1500	1505	1580	—
All-up Weight	(kg)	1900	1940	1960	—
Useful Load	(kg)	400	435	380	—
Maximum Speed	(kph)/(mph)	470/292	470/292	460/286	470/292
Cruise Speed	(kph)/(mph)	350/217	350/217	350/217	360/224
Landing Speed	(kph)/(mph)	120/75	120/75	120/75	120/75
Ceiling	(ft)	26900	26730	29520	29520
Range	(km)/(miles)	700/435	700/435	450/279	450/279
Armament		—	2 MG 17	2 – 3 MG 17	2 MG 17

Technical Data on the main Bf 109 Variants (continued)

Aircraft Type		C-1	D-1	E-1	E-3
Year of Construction		1937	1937	1938	1938
Crew		1	1	1	1
Engine		Jumo 210 G	Jumo 210 D	DB 601 A	DB 601 A
Power	PS *	700	680	1100	1100
Wingspan	(m)	9.90	9.90	9.90	9.90
Length	(m)	3.70	8.70	8.76	8.76
Height	(m)	2.45	2.45	2.45	2.45
Wing Area	(m²)	16.35	16.35	16.35	16.35
Empty Weight	(kg)	—	—	2010	2060
All-up Weight	(kg)	2170	2170	2505	2610
Useful Load	(kg)	—	—	495	550
Maximum Speed	(kph)/(mph)	470/292	460/286	537/333	570/354
Cruise Speed	(kph)/(mph)	360/224	355/220	375/234	380/236
Landing Speed	(kph)/(mph)	120/75	120/75	130/81	130/81
Ceiling	(ft)	31160	31160	36080	36080
Range	(km)/(miles)	450/279	450/279	560/348	560/348
Armament		4 MG 17	4 MG 17	4 MG 17 later 2 MG 17 + 2 MG/FF	2 MG 17 3/2 MG/FF

Aircraft Type		F-1	F-4	G-1	T-2
Year of Construction		1941	1941	1942	1940
Crew		1	1	1	1
Engine		DB 601 N	DB 601 E	DB 605 A-1	DB 601 N
Power	PS *	1175	1350	1475	1175
Wingspan	(m)	9.92	9.92	9.92	11.08
Length	(m)	8.85	8.94	9.05	8.76
Height	(m)	2.60	2.60	2.60	2.60
Wing Area	(m²)	16.20	16.20	16.20	17.50
Empty Weight	(kg)	1960	2255	2700	2250
All-up Weight	(kg)	2750	2980	3150	3080
Useful Load	(kg)	790	725	450	830
Maximum Speed	(kph)/(mph)	630/391	635/394	623/387	570/354
Cruise Speed	(kph)/(mph)	528/328	530/329	525/326	475/295
Landing Speed	(kph)/(mph)	130/81	130/81	130/81	125/78
Ceiling	(ft)	39360	38050	38540	34440
Range	(km)/(miles)	710/441	650/404	725/450	700/435
Armament		2 MG 17 1 MG/FFM	1 MG 151 2 MG 17	2 MG 17 1 MG 151/20	2 MG/FF 2 MG 17

Technical Data on the main Bf 109 Variants (continued) and Projects

Aircraft Type		G-6	G-10	K-4/R6	K-6
Year of Construction		1942	1944	1944	1944/45
Crew		1	1	1	1
Engine		DB 605 A	DB 605 D	DB 605 D	DB 605 D
Power	PS *	1475	1435	1435	1435
WIngspan	(m)	9.92	9.92	9.97	9.97
Length	(m)	8.94	8.85	9.05	9.05
Height	(m)	2.60	2.50	2.60	2.60
WIng Area	(m²)	16.02	16.10	16.05	16.05
Empty Weight	(kg)	2680	—	2346	2346
All-up Weight	(kg)	3200	3678	3383	3627
Useful Load	(kg)	520	—	1037	1281
Maximum Speed	(kph)/(mph)	630/391	685/425	710/441	700/435
Cruise Speed	(kph)/(mph)	520/323	525/326	645/401	640/397
Landing Speed	(kph)/(mph)	140/87	145/90	150/93	156/97
Ceiling	(ft)	39690	39360	40020	38700
Range	(km)/(miles)	650/404	640/397	645/401	640/397
Equipment		Various kits and field modification kits, GM1 or MW50			
Armament		2 MG 131	2 MG 131	2 MG 131	2 MG 131
		1 MG 151/20	1 MK 108	1 MK 108	1 MK 103/108

Aircraft Type		Z-1	H-1	TL	Me/Bv 155
Year of Construction		19 /	1943/44	Proj. 1943	1943/44
Crew		2	1	1	1
Engine		DB 601 E	DB 605 A-1	Jumo 004 B	DB 603 A
Power	PS *	2 x 1350	1475	2 x 880 kp	1750
Wingspan	(m)	13.27	11.92	12.55	20.50
Length	(m)	8.04	9.05	9.50	12.00
Height	(m)	3.52	2.60	2.90	3.03
Wing Area	(m²)	23.20	—	—	39.00
Empty Weight	(kg)	4900	—	3070	4869
All-up Weight	(kg)	6755	3800	4750	5521
Useful Load	(kg)	1855	—	1680	652
Maximum Speed	(kph)/(mph)	690/428	750/466	980/609	690/428
Cruise Speed	(kph)/(mph	625/388	—/—	840/522	645/401
Landing Speed	(kph)/(mph)	150/93	140/87	160/99	135/84
Ceiling	(ft)	36080	47890	36080	55600
Range	(km)/(miles)	1995/1240	625/388	1000/621	1695/1053
Equipment		—	GM 1	—	TKL 15
Armament		5 MG 151	2 MG 17	2 MK 103	1 MK 108
		ETC 250	1 MK 108	2 MG 151	2 MG 151/20

Technical Data on Me 209, Me 309 and Me 609

Aircraft Type		Me 209 V4	Me 209 V5	Me 309 V1	Me 609
Year of Construction		1940	1943/44	1942	Proj.1943
Crew		1	1	1	2
Engine		DB 601 N	DB 603 G	DB 603 G	DB 605 B
Power	PS *	1175	2000	1750	2 x 2000
Wingspan	(m)	10.04	10.95	11.04	16.00
Length	(m)	7.24	9.74	9.46	9.52
Height	(m)	—	4.00	3.90	3.24
Wing Area	(m²)	—	—	16.60	26.75
Empty Weight	(kg)	—	3339	3530	6100
All-up Weight	(kg)	—	4058	4250	9930
Useful Load	(kg)	—	719	720	3830
Maximum Speed	(kph)/(mph)	—/—	678/421	733/455	685/425
Cruise Speed	(kph)/(mph)	—/—	520/323	665/413	—/—
Landing Speed	(kph)/(mph)	—/—	150/93	—/—	—/—
Ceiling	(ft)	—	36080	39360	—
Range	(km)/(miles)	—/—	600/373	1100/683	—/—
Armament		2 MG 17	2 MG 131	—	2 MK 108
		1 MK 108	2 MG 151/20	—	2000 kg B.
			1 MK 108		

The Messerschmitt Bf 109 in the Luftwaffe

In the course of development the BF 109 was flown in the following formations in its various versions: except in the case of fighter formations the Group or Wing code is added where known.

Jagdgeschwader	1	Zerstörergeschwader	1	6U +
Jagdgeschwader	2	Zerstörergeschwader	2	3M +
Jagdgeschwader	3	Zerstörergeschwader	26	U8 +
Jagdgeschwader	4	Zerstörergeschwader	52	A2 +
Jagdgeschwader	5	Zerstörergeschwader	76	M8 +
Jagdgeschwader	6			
Jagdgeschwader	11	Lehrgeschwader	2	L2 +
Jagdgeschwader	20			
Jagdgeschwader	21	Aufklärungsgruppe	12	F3 + /H1 +
Jagdgeschwader	26	Aufklärungsgruppe	13	4E +
Jagdgeschwader	27	Aufklärungsgruppe	14	5F +
Jagdgeschwader	51	Aufklärungsgruppe	32	V7 +
Jagdgeschwader	52	Aufklärungsgruppe	100	
Jagdgeschwader	53	Aufklärungsgruppe	121	7A +
Jagdgeschwader	54	Aufklärungsgruppe	122	F6 or 5M +
Jagdgeschwader	70	Aufklärungsgruppe	123	4U +
Jagdgeschwader	71	Aufklärungsgruppe	124	G2 +
Jagdgeschwader	76			

Jagdgeschwader	77	Aufkl.Gr. d. Oberbefehlshabers d. Luftwaffe*		T5 +
Jagdgeschwader	300			
Jagdgeschwader	301	Nah-Aufkl.-Gruppe	1	
Jagdgeschwader	302	Nah-Aufkl.-Gruppe	2	
		Nah-Aufkl.-Gruppe	3	
Jagdgruppe	25	Nah-Aufkl.-Gruppe	4	
Jagdgruppe	50	Nah-Aufkl.-Gruppe	5	
Jagdgruppe	200	Nah-Aufkl.-Gruppe	8	
		Nah-Aufkl.-Gruppe	9	
Nachtjagdgruppe	10	Nah-Aufkl.-Gruppe	10	
		Nah-Aufkl.-Gruppe	11	
NachtjagdGeschwader	11	Nah-Aufkl.-Gruppe	12	
		Nah-Aufkl.-Gruppe	13	
Erprobungs-Gruppe.		Nah-Aufkl.-Gruppe	14	
later Schnellkampf-		Nah-Aufkl.-Gruppe	15	
Geschwader				
(Rapid Response Group)	210	Reserve Units/Fighter Pilot	JG 101	
		Training Schools	JG 102	
			JG 103	
			JG 104	
			JG 105	
			JG 106	
			JG 107	
			JG 108	
			JG 109	
			JG 110	
			Salzwedal	
			Altenburg	
			Delmenhorst	
			Neumünster	
			Fahrenwalde	
			Diepholz	
			Flensburg	
			Vechta	
			Wenendorf	
			Landau	

*(Reconnaissance Wing of the C-in-C Luftwaffe)

Test Centre	Rechlin	E1 + to E7 +

Glossary:

Aufklärungsgruppe	*reconnaissance wing*
Erprobungsgruppe	*test wing*
Jagdgeschwader	*fighter group*
Jagdgruppe	*fighter wing*
Lehrgeschwader	*pilot training group*
Nachtjagd-Geschwader	*night fighter group*
Nachtjagdgruppe	*night fighter wing*
Nah-Aufkl.-Gruppe	*short range reconnaissance wing*
Schnellkampf-Geschwader	*rapid response group*
Zerstörergeschwader	*Heavy fighter group*

Power Units of the Bf 109 and its Successors

Jumo 210 Liquid-cooled V-12 engine with 12 inverted cylinders
Supercharged for rated power at 11,000ft, carburettor engine
Version Da: propeller reduction drive 0.628:1
Blower ratio 7.9:1
Version Ea: as Da but blower ratio 10.5:1

DB 600 Liquid-cooled V-12 with inverted cylinders
Carburettor engine
Version C: medium pressure supercharger, propeller reduction
drive ratio 0.645
Version D: as C but propeller reduction drive ratio 0.532
Version Ga: high pressure supercharger for 13,00ft, otherwise as C

DB 601 Similar to DB 600 but fuel injection. Supercharged for 13,000ft.
Version Aa: propeller reduction drive ratio 0.645
Version Ba: propeller reduction drive ratio 0.532

DB 605 Improved DB 601 with 1475 PS take-off power, rated altitude
18,700ft.
Built under licence in Sweden and Italy
Version AM: Methanol injection for short-term power boost
Version AS: GM-1 injection system

DB 603 Larger version of DB 601 with considerably improved power
Version A, C, E = 1750 PS take-off power
Version G: take-off power increased to 2000 PS

DB 628 High altitude version of DB 605: rated altitude 36,000ft

Jumo 213 Construction similar to Jumo 210 but injection system. Like Jumo
211 but smaller. Higher rpm. Automatic 3-speed drive.
Glycol cooling. Apart from the DB 603, the most powerful
German piston engine in military service.

Power Units used in the Bf 109 and its Variants – Technical Data

Type	Length mm	Width mm	Height mm	Weight kg	Take-off power PS	rpm	Cruise power PS	rpm
Jumo 210 Da	1478	686	960	440	690	2700	550	2500
DB 600 C	1720	712	1000	555	910	2400	780	2200
DB 600 Ga	1720	712	1000	565	1050	2400	775	2200
DB 601 Aa	1722	739	1027	600	1175	2400	1000	2400
DB 605 A	2158	760	1037	751	1475	2800	1355	2800
DB 605 AM					1800	2800	1700	2800
DB 605 AS					1435	2800	1200	2800
DB 605 DC					2000	2800	1800	2800
DB 605 L					1700	2800	1350	2800
DB 603 A	2610	830	1156	910	1750	2700	1620	2700
DB 603 G	2680	830	1167	930	1900	2700	1560	2700
DB 628 A	—	—	—	860	1475	2800	1200	2800
Jumo 231 E	2070	730	920	820	1740	3000	1200	—

Junkers Jumo 210

Daimler-Benz DB 600 G

Daimler-Benz DB 601 F

Daimler-Benz DB 603 A

Daimler-Benz DB 603 U

Daimler-Benz DB 605 E

Weapons used in the Bf 109 and its Variants – Technical Data

Type	Calibre mm	Length mm	Height mm	Width mm	Weight kg	Rounds per belt	Rounds per minute	V$_O$ m/sec
MG 17	7.92	1175	159	156	10.2	500	1200	905
MG 131	13.1	1168	123	233	19.7	100	930	710/750
MG 151	15.1	1917	195	190	41.5	100	700	850/1025
Mg 151/20	20	1767	195	190	42.3	100	720	695/810
MG/FF MG/FFm	20	1338	135	155	35.7	45 – 100	540	575/700
MK 103	30	2318	348	284	145	100	420	860
MK 108	30	1057	216	222	58	100	650	520
WGr 21	210	1177	—	—	111	1	1	315
RZ 65	73	262	—	—	2.38 – 2.78	—	—	260/280

N.B: V$_O$ =   speed of exit from the weapon. This varies according to the type of ammunition in use

Weight =   weight of weapon excluding belt/drum. The MG/FF used ammunition drums of various sizes. All other weapons used disintegrating belts.

WGr & RZ   were rockets. The RZ 65 saw little active service and was only used experimentally in the Bf 109.

MK 108

MG 151/20

MG 131